TOY SOLDIERS

Series editor: Frédérique Crestin-Billet
Translated from the French by Jonathan Sly
Design by Lélie Carnot
Copyediting by Christine Schultz-Touge
Typesetting by Claude Olivier Four
Proofreading by Kate van den Boogert
Color separation by Chesteroc Graphics
Originally published as
La Folie des Petits Soldats © Éditions Flammarion, 2001
English-language edition © Éditions Flammarion, 2003
26, rue Racine
75006 Paris

03 04 05 4 3 2 1
FA1141-03-IX
ISBN: 2-0801-1141-8
Dépot légal: 09/2003

Printed in France

Collectible
TOY SOLDIERS

Dominique Pascal

Flammarion

By the same author

Collectible Miniature Cars
Éditions Flammarion
(2002)

Collectible Pocket Knives
Éditions Flammarion
(2001)

Objets de chasse à collectionner
Éditions MDM
(1999)

Objets de l'automobile à collectionner
Éditions MDM
(1998)

Objets de pêche à collectionner
Éditions MDM
(1997)

There was, at a dime store on a neighboring avenue, a window display especially for toy soldiers. At the time, the display was just too high for a ten-year-old boy like me; the gray overalled, numbskull vendor had fixed it at a level for adult eyes. Its contents—grenadiers, paratroopers, legionnaires, North African cavalrymen— set me dreaming. It had everything. The miniature soldiers, frozen in their warrior poses, were, to my eyes, very much alive. For the least occasion—a test score less cataclysmic than the last, fleeting gloom, or a scraped knee—another toy recruit would swell my miniature ranks. How can I ever say it enough? "Thanks, Mom!"

CONTENTS

Introduction

Many a juvenile imaginary world has been fed with a passion for toy soldiers. At that short-pant-wearing age, if you receive a good grade or brave out a bout of flu, there is a reward around the corner. The prize might be a lead or aluminum toy car or soldier, or maybe two. For children born during the fifties and after, they would probably come in plastic. Children's passion for toy soldiers is not something recent. Archeologists were surprised when unearthing the tomb of Prince Emsah (twelfth dynasty) in Siout, Upper Egypt, to find a collection of multicolored, wooden soldiers depicting Abyssinians and Egyptians. This is the first known collection of its kind and was buried alongside the dignitary, some four thousand years ago.

The prince, however, was no child and the presence of the collection remains a mystery; unless, that is, toy soldiers have always been produced with grown-ups or, rather, ex-kids in mind. For centuries, mankind has used wood, earth, straw, or cloth to create objects that resemble miniature soldiers—in antiquity men modeled clay with their hands, as in South America; elsewhere, people used wood; on the ice floes, the favorite material was teeth. It took a long ride down the evolutionary scale before lead figures, exclusively of religious subjects, were produced in the Middle Ages. The subsequent switch from saint to soldier also took its time. The all-important link was the paper, or card, figure, of which there are remarkable examples in Paris' Carnavalet Museum of history. The artist Jean-Baptiste Denis Le Sueur painted flat card figurines in the eighteenth century for use in instructing the Dauphin. In his book entitled *Paper Soldiers*, Edward Ryan, an authority on the subject, explains in great detail how the soldiers, manufactured between 1776 and

1781, were first cut out then folded or affixed to a piece of wood to place them upright. The inventor of the "figurine," before the term was even coined, was chevalier Pierre-François Isnard, who produced five different series of soldiers: the whole of the French cavalry; mounted dragoons and chasseurs; the complete French military uniform panoply (with 168 pieces for this series alone); five hussar regiments; and, finally, the French gendarmerie. Pierre–François Isnard was a cavalry officer, scholar, and talented artist. With the constant evolution of printing technology, these early toy soldiers, produced largely in the eastern French town of Strasbourg, increased in popularity. More towns across the east of France started to print them; first Epinal, renowned for

Paper soldiers were printed on sheets that children cut out and nailed to a small block of soft wood. The nail is visible on the feet of the First Empire soldier, on the facing page, and in the same position on the Zouave.

its printing traditions, then Verdun, Metz, Nancy, Tourcoing, Mulhouse, and Colmar. They spread to other towns and regions—to Narbonne in the far south, Nantes in the east, La Châtre in the southwest, Lille in the north, and Paris. Then abroad to Germany, the home of great printmakers such as George-Paul Buchner and J.A. Endterischen, both of Nuremberg. And to the United States, where they were produced by the McLoughlin brothers in Redington. And to Great Britain with Ernest Nister.

Once cut out, paper soldiers are ready for use. They are generally identified on the back, as can be seen with this pair: a 1460 King's Archer and Franc-Archer, a company formed to assist in the fight against the English occupiers of France. The upper part of the bow is damaged.

In southern Europe, Antonio Bosch and Juan Llorens manufactured them in Spain, and Remondini in Italy. The paper soldier was all the rage across Europe until they were gradually replaced by less fragile models.

Different styles, different attitudes, but the same material—paper.

– 16 –

L et us return to solid figures. Guy Devautour, a French specialist and collector of military figurines, describes their evolution thus: "At the end of the nineteenth century, lead soldiers, dating from King Henri IV's time (1589–1610), were discovered nestling on the bed of the river Seine. This discovery caused great sensation. During the same period, Henri's queen, Marie de Médicis, had three hundred "marmousets," or gargoyles, forged in silver for her son Louis XIII by the royal jeweler Nicolas Roger. In 1610, this collection was completed with lead representations of human subjects. It is conceivable that the miniature gargoyles were part of a set that the young prince played with in the privacy of his own chamber like any twentieth-century child. The figurines are not of soldiers, so were not intended to instruct the future king in the art of war.

At the end of the seventeenth century, the first tinsmiths in Germany —Heinrichsen, Allgeyer, Bergmann, and Hilpert—started producing flat toy figurines from tin called *zinnfigur,* which took the name "de Nuremberg" after the town where they were manufactured.

Alexandre Ballada had a special approach to figurines. For him, no detail was too difficult to reproduce. Models such as this are unique pieces that required much time and talent to create.

Hawkers and railroad men, booty bundled in knapsacks, would export them; the appearance of railroads around 1840 encouraged this worldwide spread. Originally, the Nuremberg toys were 2 to 8 inches (5–20 cm)-high. Some manufacturers, applying traditional German rigor to the problem, tried to standardize dimensions: 1 ⅕ inches (30 mm) for foot soldiers and 1 ⁹⁄₁₀ inches (40 mm) for cavalry figures. Others followed suit, including Bergmann and Borst, who also produced elegant lead figurines and were based in Strasbourg, France.

Toy soldiers were first sold in whole series, in wooden or cardboard boxes.

Facing page: Tin soldiers are generally of smaller dimensions than lead soldiers and fit perfectly into dioramas.

The Maison Lucotte first produced tin tableware before turning its hand to military figurines, in which it subsequently excelled.

Gradually, some manufactures made two-dimensional figurines thicker, in particular in Nuremberg and Hanover in Germany. Thus the semi-flat toy soldier was born, a compromise between the flat figurine and later solid lead soldiers resembling classical sculpture. It was after the French Revolution that the caster Charles-Florent Lucotte started sculpting solid lead toy soldiers. This technique produced three-dimensional characters, enabling a more realistic approach. In 1858, three other Parisian artisans—Cuberly, Blondel, and Gerbeau—went into partnership and created cavalry and foot soldiers from solid lead, stamped with their CBG initials. This company is still in business today, having survived

one and a half turbulent
centuries. From 1865 onwards,
Sosthème Gerbeau ran
the company using his own
name. As the business
flourished and he brought
his son into the fold,
the company name
changed accordingly
to "Gerbeau et fils."
The CBG initials became
a registered trademark
in 1874.

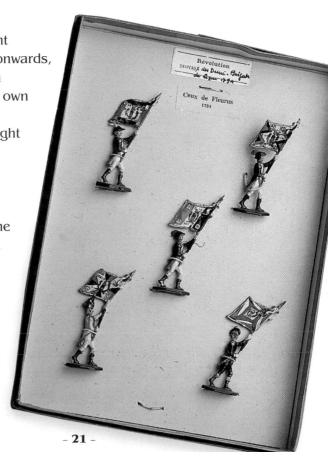

*Discovering a complete
box of toy soldiers with
its attachment wires
in place is always
a magic moment.*

The creation and production of figurines at CBG was governed by contemporary events, as was that of competitors. If newspapers reported new excavations in Greece or Egypt, vast armies of Roman legionnaries or Trojan warriors would suddenly spring forth from casters' molds. When conflict broke out in Mexico and Emperor Maximilian was executed, manufacturers' reaction was immediate, supplying stores with bushy-sideburned French soldiers and Mexican guerillas with huge moustaches. In France, the 1789 Revolution and First Empire,

The figurine world had to wait until the year 2000 and the arrival of Hervé Bernard for this model of Emperor Maximilian of Mexico, executed at Queretano on June 19, 1867.

under Napoleon, were constant sources of inspiration. Strangely, British producers took their time adopting lead soldiers. Perfidious Albion contented itself with large-scale importation of figurines from Germany and France.

It was only in 1893 that William Britain launched a lead soldier collection, which left his competition green with envy.

These American troops are in sheet metal, a material seldom used for miniatures. In the United States, toy soldiers were usually made of cast iron.

W. Britain's great idea was to manufacture hollow-cast lead soldiers. The resulting figurines used less primary materials, thereby saving money. Costs were also reduced in transportation, as the soldiers were lighter. This put serious pressure on the finest French and German casters. What was more, the British Empire reached worldwide, offering a captive market of extraordinary proportions. Its imperial army was the largest in the world with a huge diversity of uniforms, from the Bikanir in their gleaming turbans, to the Scots Guard in their busbies and motley tartan, via the dashing Bengal Lancers. Not forgetting, of course, the Royal Bahamas Police Force Band, the Canadian Mounties—with their trademark red uniforms—and, naturally, the royal family itself. William Britain was not a stranger to the toy market and, for many years, had produced moneyboxes featuring characters with articulated limbs—this idea would make all the difference. Britain's soldiers' were also articulated, meaning they could switch position. Kids at the time loved them!

Lead soldiers were either sold in boxes, paraded on plain backgrounds, as here, or on printed backgrounds, to stimulate the imagination.

Under the French Third Republic (1871–1940), lead soldier manufacturers underwent major upheavals which changed the state of play. The market was flourishing, due, unfortunately, to the proliferation of armed conflict around the globe putting new uniforms, adventures, and countries

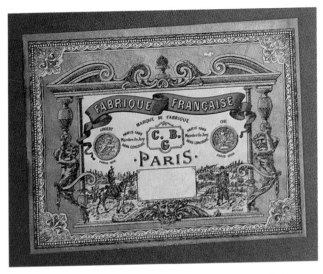

on the map.
The French public
followed the
Russo-Japanese
War (1904–05)
and Transvaal War
(1899–1902), along
with a host of other
colonial skirmishes,
in illustrated
journals such
as *L'Illustration*.
In 1904, the firm
CBG, which then belonged to Maurice Gerbeau, the son of Sosthème,
joined up with Henri Mignot. Mignot became its sole head in 1912
and added his own name to the brand. In 1928, CBG-Mignot and
Lucotte fused and the bandwagon kept rolling.

*CBG-Mignot has produced a huge number of models and varieties
in the more than one hundred years of its history. Few aspects of military
or civilian life have escaped their sculptors' attention.*

Before the Second World War, flat tin figurines were the collector's favorite. However, talented artists were also creating marvelous solid lead models. Alexandre Ballada, originally a goldsmith and jeweler, created lead soldiers in original poses. Artist André Hugo produced the Argonauts of "Golden Fleece" fame; Gaston Auger, who signed his work O.G., sculpted a series of Louis XVI and Revolution-era standard-bearers that was so impressive you can almost see their flags flapping in the wind. Pierre Alexandre, from his modest Parisian apartment, used recycled metals to make miniature marvels. He was passionate about Louis XIII's reign (1610–43) and reproduced the common folk of Paris in miniature. Other French artisans worth mentioning are Eugène Lelièpvre, the French army's official artist; Bernard Vanot; and Fernande Métayer, the woman behind the *Petits Soldats de France* series, which were sculpted by Lucien Rousselot, Frache, Gustave Vertunni, and Josiane Desfontaines, who dressed his soldiers in fine lead-leaf. All these names added their own sign of distinction to collectible figurines.

Henri VIII, king of England 1509–47, produced by Alexandre Ballada, who was fond of characters of this period. You can see other Ballada models on pages 124, 125, and 316.

Henri VIII

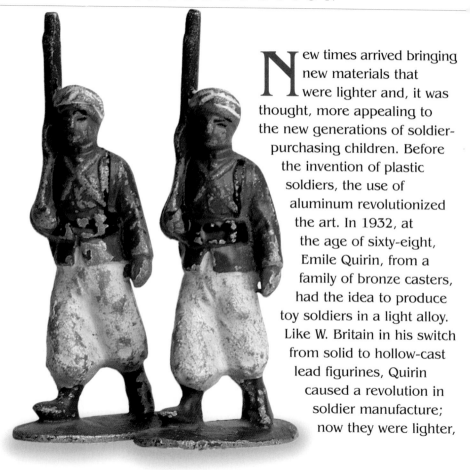

Ⓝew times arrived bringing new materials that were lighter and, it was thought, more appealing to the new generations of soldier-purchasing children. Before the invention of plastic soldiers, the use of aluminum revolutionized the art. In 1932, at the age of sixty-eight, Emile Quirin, from a family of bronze casters, had the idea to produce toy soldiers in a light alloy. Like W. Britain in his switch from solid to hollow-cast lead figurines, Quirin caused a revolution in soldier manufacture; now they were lighter, less expensive, and almost unbreakable. Naturally, the public bought even more of them and they took off instantly. Their success continued into the sixties, when trusty old aluminum was replaced by plastic, which again was lighter, less expensive to produce and transport . . . the same old story!

The Quiralu company (featured here and facing page) broke new ground marketing the first aluminum soldiers. The lightweight alloy attracted a great following from model manufacturers and was adopted by Grey-Iron and Lincoln Logs in the United States, Krolyn in Denmark, and Wend-Al in Great Britain.

The search for new modern materials is not a recent preoccupation. In 1870, celluloid was born, from the plastification of nitrocellulose by camphor, and in 1907, Bakelite replaced tortoiseshell, amber resin, and other naturally derived materials in industrial production. However, as strange as it might seem, in the United States, the Hyatt brothers had already invented plastic. Its impact later in the twentieth century would be enormous, in so many areas. But it took a while to be used in the toy-making industry. Meanwhile, research continued and imaginations ran riot, producing two fairly basic and easy to mold materials—Elastolin and a paste of plaster and flour, both of which were devised in periods of supply restrictions. The examples in this book of plaster/flour toy soldiers demonstrate their distinctive lack of finesse. Today, these figures have a certain touching charm and beauty—time has brought them soul as well as sheen.

In their day, however, given the choice between plaster/flour or lead models, a child would not have given the matter a second thought; the preference was for lead for its precision of detail.

At the start of the twentieth century, Otto and Max Hausser, doll manufacturers in

Ludwigsbourg, Germany, included in their catalogue toy soldiers
made from the same material as their dolls. The material, a mixture
of sawdust and kaolin, was called Elastolin, which subsequently
became the Hausser Brothers' brand name. Just down the road,
Oskar Wiederholz devised another composition, also including
sawdust and kaolin as well as resin and glue. Such models were
manufactured under the Lineol brand name.
The two companies' production was enormous
and covered practically all the world's armies.

*This marvelous Zouave
in action was produced
by the company Domage
et Cie, known by the
D.C. trademark.
It is made of plaster
and dates from the 1940s.*

Plastic had to wait until the end of the Second World War before it was used in figurine creation. In France, the major postwar toy soldier creator was Starlux. In 1947, the company put its first cellulose acetate models on the market. At first the figurines' uniforms were copied from 1939 uniforms. From 1955 onwards, trends dictated that uniforms should match those seen at local or national commemorative processions such as Armistice Day and Bastille Day celebrations. After World War II, the French army was summoned to the Indochina War (1945–54) and Algerian War (1954–62), conflicts that fascinated young minds— particularly those with older brothers in the Sahara or the Djebel Mountains. Starlux produced other series such as cowboys and Indians, and a superb medieval series in 1958. Their Napoleonic Empire series of 1964 received a lukewarm reception but was luckier the second time round, in 1969, the bicentenary of Napoleon's birth. In the same year, Starlux produced their first illustrated color catalogue, featuring Romans and Gauls. Meanwhile, from 1950 onwards, Pierre de Bièville launched a series of alkathene models on a smaller commercial scale. These particular figurines had a special advantage –when immersed in very hot water, the bodies, arms, and legs of characters could bend, which meant they could be manipulated into all sorts of poses. Rather than toys in the strict sense of the term, these were figurines to assemble.

Plastic toy soldiers dating from the postwar period. Plastic soldiers' low prices and imaginative designs make them very popular.

Fifteen hundred soldiers

In his memoirs, British wartime premier Sir Winston Churchill tells of his childhood passion for toy soldiers. He had fifteen hundred in all, he reckoned, all tidily classified and organized. One day, his father respectfully paid a visit to his son's room to inspect his toy troops. Lord Randolph Churchill was impressed and spent some twenty minutes contemplating the display of military strength. He then asked the young Winston if he had thought of taking up a military career. The son replied immediately in the affirmative. For years afterwards, he believed that his father had discerned burgeoning leadership qualities and pure military genius in him. With tongue in cheek, Sir Winston explains how he found out much later that his father had only suggested the military career option because he did not believe his son capable of studying to become a lawyer.

Although many military figurines are manufactured specifically for the collectors' market, this does not dampen collectors' enthusiasm for actual toy soldiers, whether of lead, aluminum, or plastic. The motivations are diverse: a desire to rediscover childhood toys long lost in the upheavals of moving to a new house; a passion for a period of history like the Napoleonic era, colonial conquests, or the Civil War; or an interest in naval or cavalry uniforms, a specific battle, or military training academies. Whatever the theme, producing a toy soldier or figurine requires two kinds of artisan —one to sculpt; the other to paint. It is difficult to dispense with the sculptor but it is possible to buy plain figurines for do-it-yourself decoration. As concerns the artists, the figurine world has a host of outstanding artists who, skillfully and prodigiously, manage to transfer the slightest details to costumes, breathing life into the models. The following pages mainly feature toy soldiers that were marketed for children. They were not made to gather

To ensure compatibility between models, the heights of toy soldiers were generally standardized from the middle of the XIXth century onwards. The height of a toy soldier is measured from the top of its base to its eyes. For a cavalier, the height is measured from beneath the horse's hooves to the figure's eyes. From right to left, these figures' heights are 3 inches (80 mm), 2 ¼ inches (60 mm) and 1 ½ inches (35 mm).

dust on a shelf but to be deployed in unforgettable bedroom-floor battles that only a child and his—or sometimes her—imagination can wage. Of course, the desire to play toy soldiers may return at any time, decades later, along with the desire to collect and arrange them, parading in regimental lines, frozen in motion but still very much alive in your own heart.

This figurine, marketed without paint by Le Cimier, was interpreted on the left by Guilien and on the right by Stéphane Charvet, two figurine artists with a keen interest in history.

Here are two Polish Chevau-Légers drummers of the Imperial Guard: the one on the left was decorated as a figurine by Russian Vitaz, and the one on the right was produced as a toy by CBG-Mignot. Each to his own taste.

I

FLAT
toy soldiers

It took just a piece of engraved slate, or another readily workable material, to cast a flat tin figurine barely as thick as a slip of cardboard. Such models amused children for over a century. *Zinnfiguren* were invented in Nuremburg, Germany, at the end of the eighteenth century with two kinds of clients in mind: children, drawn to simply decorated forms, and adults with a passion for military art, attracted by the elaborate workmanship of skillful artists. Little by little, flat tin figurines took on volume and became semi-flat models, before they in turn became the "real" solid lead soldiers that are so much a part of our collective memory. We will deal with the latter in the next chapter.

Flat lead soldier from the Second Empire in France (1852–70). Here are both sides of the same figurine: the front on the left, the back on the right. Unknown manufacturer.

*Two flat tin models
of infantry soldiers,
standing to attention,
from the reign
of Louis-Philippe
(1830–48).
They were no doubt
manufactured
by Blondel et fils,
tinsmiths in Paris
from 1839 onwards.*

A First Empire lancer in flat tin. The manufacturer is unknown, but possibly from Strasbourg.

This flat tin Austrian infantry soldier exudes an indisputable charm. Its unusually proportioned small head and large body give it a resolute allure, while the raised leg lends an uncanny sense of movement. Toy soldiers of this era were often depicted standing to attention. In Christian Blondieau's book (bottom, page 103), there is a 2 ⅘ inch (70 mm)-high drum major, attributed to Cherchie, with the same small-headed, large-bodied characteristics.

Whether this cavalier is German or Austrian is unclear. What is certain is that it dates from before 1840. Precision in uniform detail developed over time but for some toys, like this flat tin model, a certain freedom was allowed.

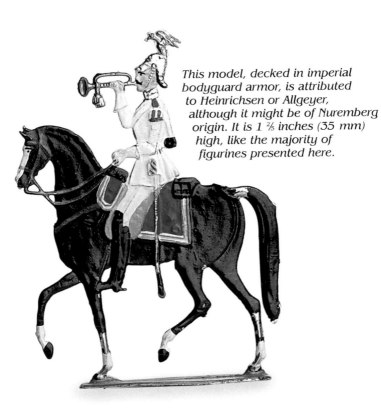

This model, decked in imperial bodyguard armor, is attributed to Heinrichsen or Allgeyer, although it might be of Nuremberg origin. It is 1 ⅖ inches (35 mm) high, like the majority of figurines presented here.

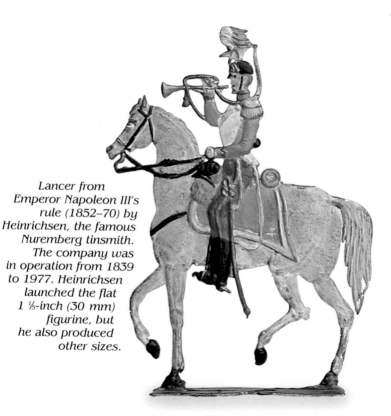

Lancer from Emperor Napoleon III's rule (1852–70) by Heinrichsen, the famous Nuremberg tinsmith. The company was in operation from 1839 to 1977. Heinrichsen launched the flat 1 ⅕-inch (30 mm) figurine, but he also produced other sizes.

Another Third Empire lancer attributed to Heinrichsen. Note that most models at the beginning of this chapter have been enlarged (two or threefold) to allow more details to be seen.

These Danish grenadiers, dating from the second part of the nineteenth century, carrying their rifles on the left, are easily identifiable by their red coats. The manufacturer is unknown.

A delightful flat tin model depicting a hussar from the French Revolutionary era. The manufacturer's name, here unknown, was sometimes engraved on the sabretache. Note his "mirliton," a form of shako covered in fabric.

*These fifteenth-century knights
in tournament regalia display two aspects
typical to Nuremberg craftsmanship.
The one on the right measures more than
4 inches (100 mm) high, whereas the one
on the left is 1 ⅖ inches (35 mm).
At the time, producers were still
manufacturing models using
their own dimensions.*

This knight was probably made by Carl Ludwig Besold, of Nuremberg, whose company was taken over by the Hafner brand in 1893. The molds were recycled and the two models were recently reproduced.

*A typical Heinrichsen vignette. The company liked to
compose scenic themes with groups of soldiers.
The Heinrichsen dynasty lasted for over a century.
Note the fine quality of the engraving.*

Contemporary flat tin model inspired by Jacques Louis David's famous painting of Napoleon Bonaparte crossing the Alps in 1796, during the prelude to the Italian campaign.

*Dromedary regiment
officer from the 1899
French campaign
in Egypt. It is part of
a particularly beautiful
series of figurines,
produced by Wimor
(signed on the base),
of which there is another
example on the facing page.*

General Napoleon Bonaparte's expedition party to Egypt included a number of scholars, a theme that inspired many figurine manufacturers. The traveling academics were often the brunt of soldiers' jokes. Here, one is seen asking for help to dismount. The journeying intellectuals included such figures as the chemist Claude Berthollet, the mathematician Gaspard Monge, and the physician Nicolas Conté.

Here, a Mameluke is seen proudly carrying the sheik's emblematic battle banner: a long horse tail resembling a flame. The model was made by Segom, a producer of figurines in plastic . . .

. . . (see pages 66 and 311), who also imported tin models. This is a semi-flat figurine. Below is the flipside of the same figurine.

*French and German manufacturers
such as CBG and Heinrichsen,
respectively, have produced a
good number of decors.
These burning ruins
are the same
scale as 1 ⅖ inch
(35 mm)–high soldiers.*

General Lassalle always charged, as the legend goes, pipe in hand. He was fond of saying: "A hussar who isn't dead at thirty is a blackguard." He himself was killed at the Battle of Wagram (July 6, 1809) at the age of thirty-three.

The emperor is on the left; on the right, a light cavalry chasseur of the Imperial Guard. This model is attributed to Heinrichsen and is 1 ⁶⁄₁₀ inches (40 mm) high.

*In the foreground, the Emperor Napoleon is seen
galloping with his general officers. Behind him
is the marshal of the empire, Jozef Poniatowski.
This technically elegant, flat tin model was made
by Heinrichsen; the figures are affixed to the base
by six legs instead of sixteen.*

This Russian soldier, a tin standard-bearer from the Napoleonic era, was probably produced by Segom at the start of the 1960s.

This Italian cuirassier was manufactured by Schweizer—a tinsmith in Ammersee, Germany, from the middle of the nineteenth century onwards.

Figurine artists are not only inspired by great victories but also by illustrious defeats. This model, with its touch of realism, was made by Heinrichsen in the 1920s and depicts Napoleon at the Battle of Waterloo, June 18, 1815. It depicts the emperor's troops advising him to leave the battlefield, which is strewn with bodies, including that of an English soldier on the left.

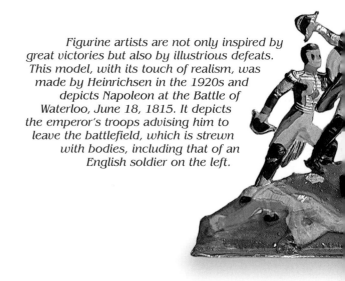

This officers' mess is attributed to Krause and dates from the 1860s. It depicts France's famous Châlons-sur-Marne military drill camp that was often depicted by French and foreign manufacturers.

An Austrian, his lance high, facing a charging German lancer. The German is a semi-flat model. By the shape of the extended base, it can probably be attributed to Spenckuch, a German manufacturer.

*Life at the barracks, like life in the field camp,
was a favorite theme for manufacturers.
These semi-flat Prussian soldiers were
probably made in Germany (by Krause) . . .*

. . . At 1 ⅕ inches (30 mm), they are attractive depictions of soldiers at rest or, at least, away from the fray.

This Zouave mess scene at the Châlons training camp is also attributed to Krause. The model is semi-flat, a description that is variable and may mean flat or well-rounded relief.

Another semi-flat scene depicting the open-air canteen at the Châlons training camp. The model was cast from a single mold and dates from Napoleon III's time (1852–70). Such scenes could also be made by soldering several subjects to a metal plate.

The military camp at Châlons-sur-Marne, today called Mourmelon, was established to the east of Paris in 1859 and has since been the subject of a great many figurines. Its location near Paris meant that Parisians could visit it to watch training maneuvers. This piece is from Napoleon III's era.

German manufacturers were fond of depicting
the most prominent regiments from armies
around the world, such as these Italian
"bersaglieres." The Swiss manufacturer Verly
also sculpted them in the same style.

*Scene depicting the death of French commander
Berregier at the hands of the Prussians
in 1870. The model is a special edition
from 1920. During the twenties,
however, German interest in
military figurines waned,
turning instead towards
civilian and farm life.*

Another slice of history, a legend in foreign legion annals—the Battle of Camerone. On April 30, 1863, in Mexico, sixty-five legionnaires held out against twenty-five hundred Mexicans. Only five survived. A monument to their courage at the site reads: "Here, they were less than sixty against a whole army. Its mass crushed them but life rather than courage abandoned these French soldiers April 30, 1863."

This French cuirassier was made by Babette Schweizer, who purchased a number of nineteenth-century Nuremburg molds to reissue their designs. Note the dust kicked up by the horse's hind legs that is typical of the Nuremberg producers, Ammon and Son.

Standard-bearer officer of the French infantry, from 1870, by Babette Schweizer. The original designer of this model is unknown. Tin models could be sold with arms of different shapes, so that they could adopt different poses. Those limbs that did not suit the scene could be removed.

By comparing it to other models, the French figurine restorer Raymond Oehl attributes this 1 ⅖-inch (35 mm) battleship to a Danish craftsman, Söhlke, who was manufacturing in Hamburg.

This battleship was produced by Heinrichsen, the German figurine dynasty that attempted to standardize the heights of flat figurines.

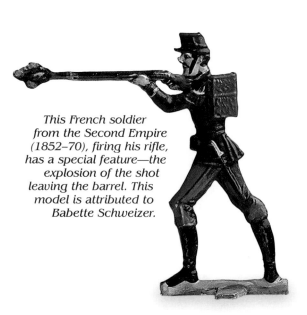

This French soldier from the Second Empire (1852–70), firing his rifle, has a special feature—the explosion of the shot leaving the barrel. This model is attributed to Babette Schweizer.

The difference between a toy soldier and a figurine depends on the degree of detail. However, time lends toy soldiers a certain charm that makes them ideal for window displays.

The mold for this 1 ⅘-inch (45 mm) semi-flat artilleryman was manufactured by the Schneider family, based in the Rhineland, Germany. They were the first to commercialize separate molds for home figurine production.

This semi-flat First World War dragoon from 1914—charging, saber drawn—was also cast from a Schneider mold. Schneider produced nearly every military unit from the First World War.

*Heinrichsen produced some very elegant
semi-flat figurines of firemen performing
their various functions. Here, they are seen
removing a sofa and, on the right, a mirror
and a side table.*

*Even firefighters had a place
in French and German manufacturers'
battle plans.*

Continuing Heinrichsen's firefighter series: a horse-drawn water tank and hose. The models on the right are moving furniture and humans to safety.

Firefighters have been a recurrent
theme for all toy soldier creators.
Here and on the facing page are semi-flat
examples, produced by CBG.
Their 1 ³⁄₁₀-inch (32 mm) height is
the manufacturer's smallest model.

The firefighters on the facing page carry axes and a bucket; here, they are depicted pushing a fire-hose reel towards the scene of the fire. This model dates from the Third Republic in France (1870–1940).

This violent scene from Napoleon III's era (1852–70) was produced by the German manufacturer Krauser. Note that German designers often model French soldiers with very narrow waists.

This accessory was produced by CBG during the French Third Republic (1870–1940) to decorate parades.

A cadet from the world famous Saint-Cyr academy, in a semi-flat style by CBG. The manufacturer initiated this technique at the end of the 1890s.

These dromedaries appeared when northern Europe was colonizing Africa and discovering its mysteries. The animal itself caused great sensation in France. The model on the right is part of a 1907 CBG set entitled "Chasse au Soudan" (Hunting in Sudan). It included a dozen human models, both black and white, and a number of animals, including a crocodile eating a black baby. The semi-flat model on the left belongs to the colonial forces and was produced in 1912.

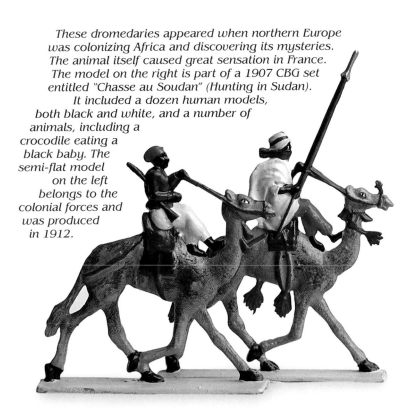

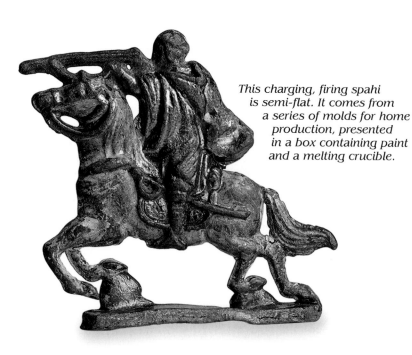

This charging, firing spahi is semi-flat. It comes from a series of molds for home production, presented in a box containing paint and a melting crucible.

For authentic Eastern scenes, palm trees were essential. A child could use such a model to build dioramas depicting African troops on maneuvers, a hunt in Sudan, or the famous Citroën "Croisière Noire" (1924–25)— when the automobile manufacturer drove one of its cars from Algeria across Africa via Kenya to the Cape of Good Hope.

*These semi-flat charging foot soldiers were
created by Lucotte. With one foot on their base,
they are 1 ⅕ to 1 ⅗ inches (30–40 mm) high and
are remarkable for their quality
of engraving and casting.*

*With semi-flat lead and flat tin models,
foot soldiers' feet and horses' hooves are held
on the same plane of the base.*

The figurine manufacturer Lucotte was among those who celebrated the arrival of American expeditionary forces to swell the Allied ranks in 1917. Thus, these semi-flat soldiers charging.

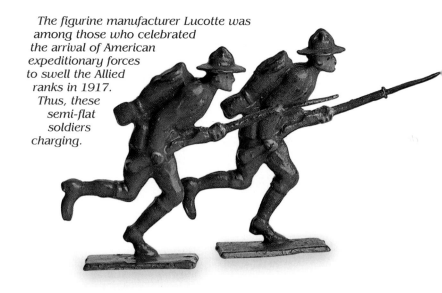

*Lucotte produced marvelous
1 %10-inch (40mm) wonders,
but they were not immediately
successful. They had
to wait several years
before collectors
latched onto models
depicting the 1914–18 war.*

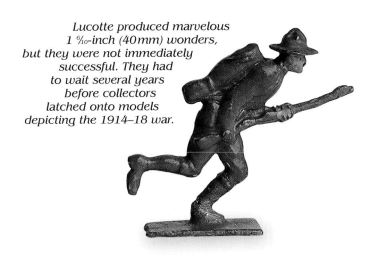

II

LEAD
toy soldiers

T he origins of lead toy soldiers go back to the Middle Ages. Their success as toys, however, took off in the second half of the nineteenth century, due to the efforts of French and German manufacturers; the British followed suit shortly afterwards. New-found affluence and forms of transport such as railroads helped widen toy factories' horizons. The century's industrial revolution was highly productive, giving birth to new, totally futile needs. The lead soldier was just such a need.

The orders of knighthood were created in the Middle Ages, throughout Europe, at the time of the Crusades. Spain had the Calatrava and Alcantara Orders; Portugal, the Avis Order; and Germany, the Teutonic Order. This is a knight of the Order of Saint John, produced for the French store Les Drapeaux de France.

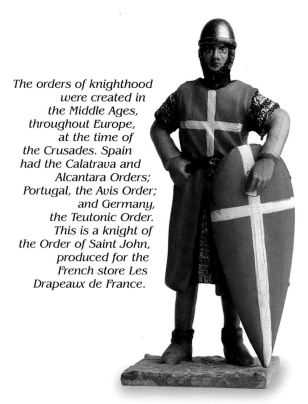

This model was also produced for the store Les Drapeaux de France. This knight of the Order of Malta is identifiable by the trademark red cross on his chest. The Order of Malta emerged from an order established in 1099 by the Hospitallers of Saint John of Jerusalem. The knights took refuge in Malta from 1518 to 1798 when Napoleon Bonaparte occupied the island.

Joan of Arc, also known as the Maid of Orleans, is a common lead model. She was born in Domrémy, in the east of France, in 1412; in 1429, at the head of her small army, she conquered the English occupiers at the Battle of Patay, south of Paris. She was executed in Rouen on May 30, 1431. This action figurine was produced by a British craftsman, Richard Courtenay.

Another Joan of Arc figurine, produced by CBG-Mignot, who have introduced a number of models of her throughout their long history. A striking example is their 1894 version of the Maid of Orleans riding a caparisoned horse. Joan was beatified in 1909 and canonized in 1920.

The British craftsman
Richard Courtenay, a former
student of the prestigious Ecole
des Beaux Arts in Paris, was
a great specialist of chivalry.
From 1928 to 1963,
he produced superb
figurines, like this
fatally injured
man in armor.

Richard Courtenay had the foresight to create knights with removable helmets, such as this eloquent model of a knight in battle. The figure could be Jean Rocourt at the Battle of Poitiers, Guy Rochefort, or Sir Edward Courtenay—models of whom, and many others besides, Richard Courtenay produced.

The traditional halberds of these knights on foot are less than straight due to the suppleness of the lead. The models were produced by CBG at the end of the nineteenth century. The halberd, with its spearhead tip and two sharp edges, is a polearm, the generic term for all weapons fixed to a pole.

*This halberdier was cast in lead
from a plastic figurine mold.
The model was produced for
the coffee brand Mokarex,
who slipped free 1 ⅘ or
2 ⅖-inch (45 or 60 mm)
silver or gold painted plastic
figurines into their packets of
coffee to arouse collectors'
passions. They touched on
a number of themes: the Middle
Ages, the Musketeers, the "Grand
Siècle" of Louis XIV's reign
(1643–1715), the Napoleonic
Empire, and others. All in all,
more than three hundred
characters were issued.*

Courtenay, from Slough in England, also produced this model of Bertrand du Guesclin, constable of France during the early part of the Hundred Years' War (1377–1453). Born near Dinan in the north of France, he died in 1380 at the siege of Châteauneuf-de-Randon.

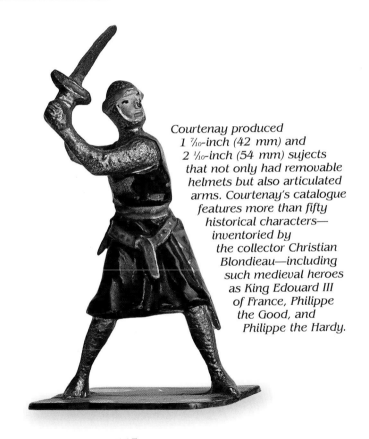

Courtenay produced
1 ⁷⁄₁₀-inch (42 mm) and
2 ¹⁄₁₀-inch (54 mm) sujects
that not only had removable
helmets but also articulated
arms. Courtenay's catalogue
features more than fifty
historical characters—
inventoried by
the collector Christian
Blondieau—including
such medieval heroes
as King Edouard III
of France, Philippe
the Good, and
Philippe the Hardy.

Tradition is a recent
English brand name
that has produced
a number of
medieval subjects.
Here is Humphrey
Littleburg, painted
by figurine
artist Guilien.
The model on
the facing page
was painted
by Sylvette.

Edward, Earl of Grandpré, at Agincourt, October 25, 1415—the famous battle where the French suffered a heavy defeat at the hands of the English.

The creator of this model is unknown. This fifteenth-century French archer is a good example of the many poses dreamed up by figurine manufacturers to make their soldiers lifelike.

As may already be apparent, Richard Courtenay was not fond of static poses—witness this French king, Jean II Le Bon, in combat. His stance, the broken sword, and the movement in his tunic lend him great realism.

The store Les Drapeaux de France had a number of flags on offer, including this Saxe regiment standard from the former eastern German state that encompassed the towns of Leipzig, Dresden, and Zwickau, and which provided the French king, Louis XV, with troops.

*Another Louis XV
military standard,
produced by the
Spanish brand Pegaso
and painted
by Sylvette.*

*This standard belongs
to the Walloon Guard
who served the king
of Spain from 1702
onwards. It has a lead
body and metal sheet flag and
was designed by Guy Renaud, who
has produced historical figurines
from his base in Tours, France,
since 1957.*

GARDES WALLONNES

French manufacturer Guy Renaud's specialty is regimental flags from the reigns of Louis XIV, XV, and XVI, and even the First Republic. This standard belonged to the district of Saint-Honoré, which was one of the new districts of Paris following the Revolution.

57. DISTRICT DE St HONORE

This Napoleonic
Empire aide-de-camp
is a rarity. It was
hand-painted by
Alexandre Ballada
in the 1940s
or 1950s.

This hussar from the revolutionary era is also by Ballada. Both are made of lead and coated with tin leaf. They measure 2 ¹⁄₁₀ inches (54 mm).

The fife player is wearing a morion helmet and the drummer a "bouquingan" cap. Both these musicians were made by the figurine artist Pierre Alexandre, who supplied French actors Sacha Guitry, Noël Noël, and Fernand Gravey with toy soldiers.

Musketeers are by definition soldiers armed with muskets. Note the forked support, enabling the musketeer to shoot without moving. These models were also produced by Pierre Alexandre, in the middle of the twentieth century.

This officer and grenadier of the French Imperial Guard of 1870 were inspired from Edouard Detaille's and Alphonse de Neuville's vast panorama of the Battle of Rezonville, August 16, 1870.

Like the soldiers on the facing page, Hervé Bernard used historical documentation to design this captain and volunteer of the Chouans, an army of royalist insurgents in the west of France, from Year II (1793–94) of the French Revolution. They are made of lead and are 2 ¹⁄₁₀ inches (54 mm) high.

Paris was divided into sixty districts according to a decree of April 15, 1789. Each corresponded to a juridical area. After the Revolution, the twenty-eighth district became known as "Les Enfants Rouges" (The Red Children). This figurine was produced by Guy Renaud.

28. DISTRICT DES ENFANTS ROUGES

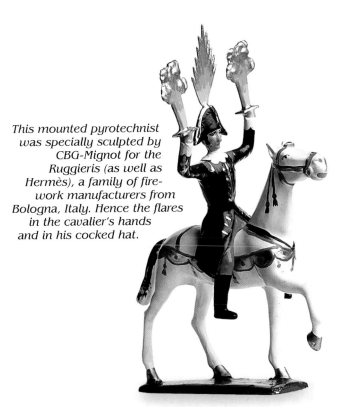

This mounted pyrotechnist was specially sculpted by CBG-Mignot for the Ruggieris (as well as Hermès), a family of fire-work manufacturers from Bologna, Italy. Hence the flares in the cavalier's hands and in his cocked hat.

The French Guard,
created under the reign
of Charles XI, are here
seen wearing their
Louis XIV–era uniform.
They were essentially
a municipal police
force, responsible for
maintaining order.
It is also believed they
played the role of
"procurers" to the
"ladies" of Paris.

The French Guard were dressed in blue, and the Swiss Guard wore red uniforms. The Swiss Guard were usually assigned to the king but if necessary would go into battle. These models were made recently by CBG-Mignot from antique molds.

The "Royal Italien" were actually a French regiment belonging to King Louis XV. The troop originally consisted of Italian nationals and the name was retained even when their numbers dwindled. This model was made by Guy Renaud.

ROYAL ITALIEN

Les Drapeaux de France was a famous lead soldier manufacturer and boutique, outside the Palais-Royal in Paris. It was run by Jacques Bittard from the end of the Second World War until 1986. Strollers could wander along the adjacent Montpensier gallery and watch the craftsman fashioning his figurines. He specialized in small vignettes, featuring one or two characters, such as this grenadier of the guard of 1808, presenting the regimental standard.

Grenadiers de la Garde 1808

Perched relatively far back on his horse, this cuirassier drummer was made by CBG-Mignot. The first Mamelukes were introduced into France from Egypt during the empire and were generally black.

This Mameluke trumpeter—also part of the CBG-Mignot collection—seated on a saddle bearing the imperial gold eagle insignia, is a contemporary reproduction. The Mamelukes were troops from a joint Turkish-Egyptian army, originally made up of slaves who subsequently became part of the ruling elite of Egypt.

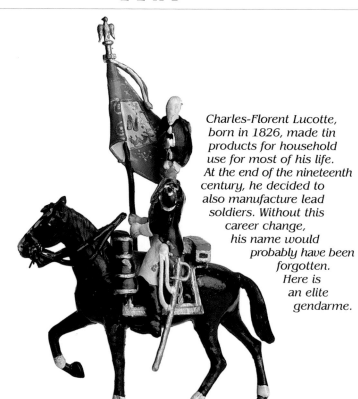

*Charles-Florent Lucotte,
born in 1826, made tin
products for household
use for most of his life.
At the end of the nineteenth
century, he decided to
also manufacture lead
soldiers. Without this
career change,
his name would
probably have been
forgotten.
Here is
an elite
gendarme.*

This superb Napoleonic officer of the seventh hussar regiment, bearing a standard mounted with the emperor's trademark gold eagle, was made by Guy Renaud of Tours, France. On his left shoulder is his pelisse, thrown on to protect from saber blows in combat.

Gustave Vertunni was born in Rome in 1884. Before his death in Paris in 1953, he produced hundreds of historical characters, including Napoleonic generals and French royalty. This model is of General Joachim Mural, born in Labastide-Murat in 1767, who married Caroline Bonaparte. He was king of Naples from 1808 to 1815, the year in which he was shot dead in Pizzo, Italy.

Another Gustave Vertunni model: Count Philibert Sérurier, a general of the French army (1742–1819). He was born in Laon in the north of France and was also governor of the ex-serviceman's home, the Hôtel des Invalides in Paris.

As well as famous characters, Gustave Vertunni also produced lead figurines of soldiers bedecked in their immaculate uniforms. Here is an artillery colonel of the Imperial Guard.

This light cavalry chasseur of the Imperial Guard is also by Gustave Vertunni. This figurine, like that on the facing page, was manufactured between 1935 and 1950. After the death of her husband, Vertunni's widow continued casting the more basic models. These have glossier paint than those produced in Gustave's time.

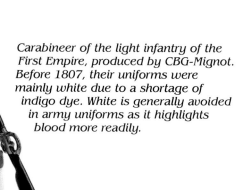

Carabineer of the light infantry of the
First Empire, produced by CBG-Mignot.
Before 1807, their uniforms were
mainly white due to a shortage of
indigo dye. White is generally avoided
in army uniforms as it highlights
blood more readily.

These three Austrian artillery gunners from
the First Empire are carrying the tools
of their gunning trade. From left to right
is the shot firer who lights the wick,
the cannonball bearer, and finally
the sponge carrier—the instrument
used to clean the cannon after firing.
The models are recent reproductions
manufactured by CBG-Mignot
from antique molds.

Under the First Empire,
soldiers' uniforms were
the same on the battlefield
as on the parade ground.
Thus, in 1810, an officer
of the light infantry would
have worn this uniform
to battle, even though it
seems more suitable
for evening wear than
the chaos of war.
The role of the infantry
in warfare has been central
throughout the ages.
This model was produced
by CBG-Mignot.

First Empire musicians were permitted to wear more colorful uniforms than other soldiers. The actual choice of color was left to the discretion of the commanding colonel. This is a model of a musician of the seventeenth chasseur regiment, manufactured by CBG-Mignot.

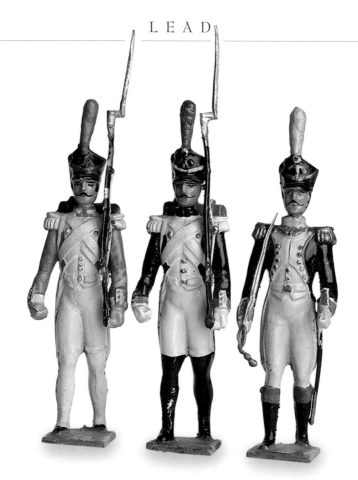

MIM, a Belgian company established in Brussels by Emmanuel Steinback, is no longer in existence. Between 1935 and 1948, it produced figurines that are identifiable by their 2 ⅖-inch (60 mm) height and square bases. These three examples are part of a fusilier-grenadier company and may have belonged to "Iron Marshal" Davout's first division. On the right is an officer with his characteristic boots and saber; on the left are two foot soldiers bearing their weapons.

A Polish drummer of the Grand-Duchy of Warsaw infantry that served France during the First Empire. He is wearing the famous "chapska" hat. Note that Polish uniforms were mainly red. Dutch attire was similar but predominantly blue. Manufactured by CBG-Mignot.

The standard is always borne by an officer, an honor usually reserved for the one with the most medals. Here is a French light infantry officer from 1810. The three-striped, tricolor flag only appeared in 1812.

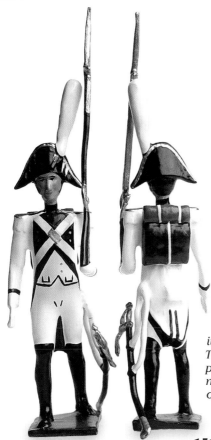

This model viewed from both front and back depicts the Strasbourg Guard of Honor from the First Empire era. In big cities, the affluent middle classes would buy their sons beautiful uniforms when they enrolled in such regiments. Thus predisposed to army life, they would join the imperial army whenever it passed through town. These are recent CBG-Mignot productions based on models from the beginning of the twentieth century.

A light cavalry chasseur bugler from the Imperial Guard manufactured by CBG-Mignot. Note the sabretache, next to the saber—decorated with the trademark gold eagle imperial insignia on the side—in which aides-de-camp would carry letters. Napoleon I would always dispatch three officers with the same missive so that at least one would reach his destination.

The horse grenadiers are descendants of the French Royal Guard. They distinguished themselves particularly at the Battle of Eylau. During the battle, it is said that they initially ducked their heads to avoid oncoming bullets, until their commander, General Lepic, said to them: "Raise your heads, men! It's grapeshot! Not shit!" Manufactured by CBG-Mignot.

CBG-Mignot manufactured these figures of a light infantry grenadier standard-bearer and soldier. The grenadiers were created in 1667 in France and were made up of four brigades. Grenadier units ceased to feature in the French army after 1870. According to the Larousse dictionary, the term "grenadier" in French also refers to a tall woman of a daring disposition.

Population figures help explain France's domination of Europe during the First Empire. While Russia had a population of thirty-six million, England had six million and France, twenty-six million. This infantry officer and standard-bearer were produced by CBG-Mignot.

A superb charging First Empire Austrian hussar. The army would try anything to unnerve the enemy. The plume on this hussar's "colback," a form of truncated fur busby, made each soldier appear larger, so more dangerous to the enemy.

The cavaliers of the Prussian Guard would provocatively sharpen their sabers on the steps of the French embassy in Berlin. Manufactured by CBG-Mignot.

As well as throwing their pelisses over their shoulders, cavaliers would grow sideburns that they would braid to protect themselves from saber thrusts. Similarly, hussars would often wear their hair long at the back in a plait. Manufactured by CBG-Mignot.

Grenadiers of the Imperial Guard in full parade regalia. Here they are wearing culottes, whereas they would have worn pants for marching. Although they did appear on the battlefield, they stayed in the back lines and it is said other battalions disliked them intensely. Manufactured by CBG-Mignot.

This flag featuring
a two-headed eagle
from the time of
the First Empire may
have belonged to
the Russians, Prussians,
or Austrians. This pair
are in fact Austrians—
a drummer and
a standard-bearer
on parade. Manufactured
by CBG-Mignot.

The headwear of these Russians
in action is interesting—
the miter was also worn
by the English army from
the seventeenth
century onwards.
The soldiers
are equipped
with standard-issue sabers
and rifles fitted with bayonets.
Manufactured by CBG-Mignot.

*This light infantry chasseur
musician might have been
a draftee in the French army,
as conscription was
introduced in 1790.
The fife player marched
at the head of army
battalions, wearing
a distinctive uniform,
to impress the prospective
enemy as well as to encourage
new recruits with a soft spot for
uniforms. This model, as well as
the drum major on the facing
page, was manufactured
by CBG-Mignot.*

Grenadier drum majors of the Imperial Guard were selected for their height. During the First Empire, the minimum requirement was 6 foot 6 inches (2 m) so they could launch their batons even higher. It is said that when parading beneath the triumphal Arc du Carrousel, they would launch their batons skywards on one side, then catch them again on the other. A likely story!

This recent Metal Models figurine depicts a brigadier of the African chasseurs of the fourth Crimean regiment. The Crimean War (1854–56) was fought, at Sebastopol, between the Russians and a coalition of Turkey, France, England, and Piedmont.

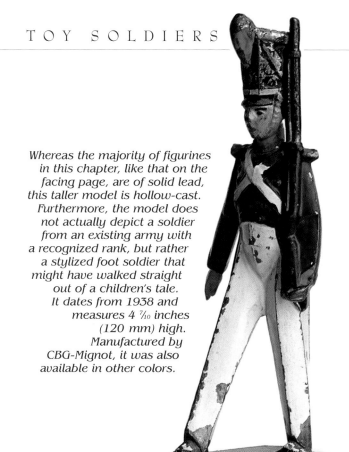

Whereas the majority of figurines in this chapter, like that on the facing page, are of solid lead, this taller model is hollow-cast. Furthermore, the model does not actually depict a soldier from an existing army with a recognized rank, but rather a stylized foot soldier that might have walked straight out of a children's tale. It dates from 1938 and measures 4 ⁷⁄₁₀ inches (120 mm) high. Manufactured by CBG-Mignot, it was also available in other colors.

The Janissaries were an elite troop under the command of the sultan of Istanbul and fought against the Russians and Austrians at the end of the eighteenth century. This British-made figurine by Tradition depicts a Turkish corporal.

Metal Models are manufacturers of lead soldiers that are magnificently sculpted by a contemporary figurine artist by the name of Leibovitz, who made this Zouave (from 1854–56). The word Zouave comes from "zwâwa," the name of a Kabylian tribe. The French Zouaves were founded in 1831. Another Metal Models figurine is featured on page 164.

Egypt and the Sudan were once part of the same country under British protectorate. Here is a Sudanese drummer of the English army produced by CBG-Mignot, from the start of the twentieth century onwards.

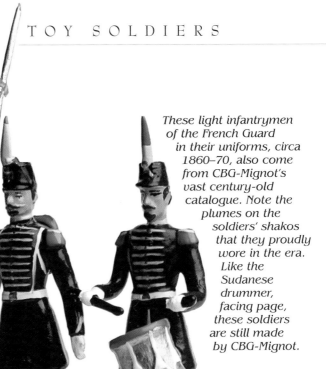

These light infantrymen of the French Guard in their uniforms, circa 1860–70, also come from CBG-Mignot's vast century-old catalogue. Note the plumes on the soldiers' shakos that they proudly wore in the era. Like the Sudanese drummer, facing page, these soldiers are still made by CBG-Mignot.

This Bengal lancer, wearing his characteristic turban, was made in England. Note the lance crowned with the regiment's own pennon.

The Bengal lancer on the facing page is unusual for a CBG-Mignot model as it has no base, unlike this Chinese cavalier from the era of the Boxer Rebellion in 1900. As lead is a particularly soft metal, it loses its shape easily, possibly unbalancing the toy.

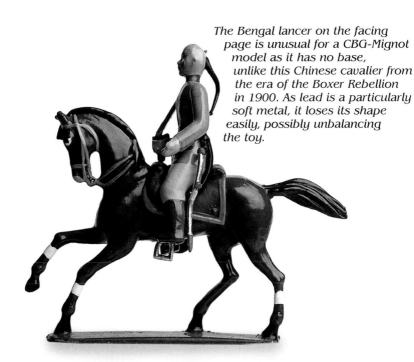

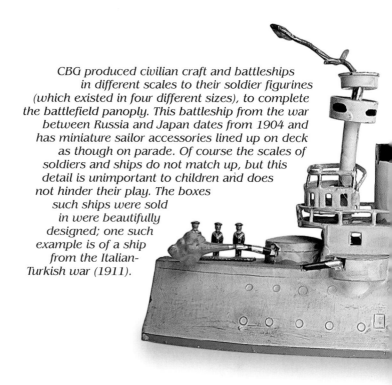

*CBG produced civilian craft and battleships
in different scales to their soldier figurines
(which existed in four different sizes), to complete
the battlefield panoply. This battleship from the war
between Russia and Japan dates from 1904 and
has miniature sailor accessories lined up on deck
as though on parade. Of course the scales of
soldiers and ships do not match up, but this
detail is unimportant to children and does
not hinder their play. The boxes
such ships were sold
in were beautifully
designed; one such
example is of a ship
from the Italian-
Turkish war (1911).*

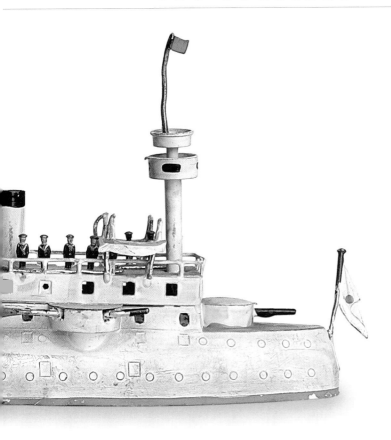

This proud British soldier, mounted on his dromedary, is a souvenir of the Sudanese campaign from the end of the nineteenth century. He is wearing the characteristic colonial helmet, which is still issued in the British army. The model is contemporary and made in England.

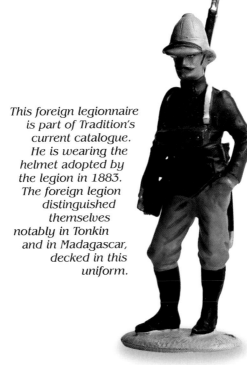

This foreign legionnaire is part of Tradition's current catalogue. He is wearing the helmet adopted by the legion in 1883. The foreign legion distinguished themselves notably in Tonkin and in Madagascar, decked in this uniform.

These Arab auxiliaries were very popular at the end of the nineteenth and start of the twentieth century. The long weapon belonging to the one on the right resembles a "miquelet" rifle. The soldier on the right, however, is armed only with a stick. Made by CBG.

The French colonialization of Algeria took place between 1830 and 1847. This figurine depicts a spahi of the colonial troops. Produced by CBG and still available.

The United States set out to free Cuba
from Spanish control and dispatched
an expeditionary force called
the "Rough Riders." The Hispania brand
recreated the Cuban episode with a series
that included these two Spanish soldiers.

Fidel Castro and Che Guevara were not the first to make the beard fashionable in Havana. This Spanish sailor might have seen his national fleet destroyed by the American army.

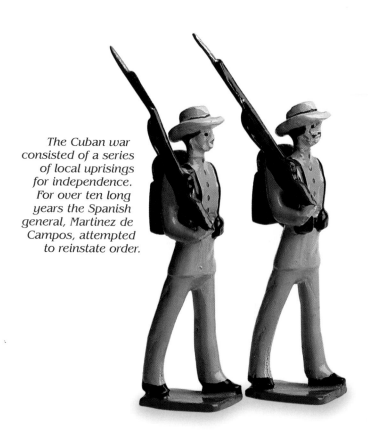

The Cuban war consisted of a series of local uprisings for independence. For over ten long years the Spanish general, Martinez de Campos, attempted to reinstate order.

This parading standard-bearer, carrying the red and yellow Spanish flag, was produced—like the foot soldiers on the facing page—by the Hispania brand.

Children reading illustrated magazines at the end of the nineteenth century had access to scenes of great military violence, such as that of the China war. A good many Chinese military figurines emerged from the conflict. From 1894 onwards, CBG marketed this infantryman along with other vignettes, including one of a decapitation by saber.

The long mustaches and slanted eyes are a giveaway: these are Chinese soldiers from the Boxer Rebellion. They were not made by CBG, however; their finish is glossier, more typical of British brands.

These line infantrymen on parade were made by CBG under Gerbeau's management. Their bodies were adaptable for other armies. The molds only needed slight modification to minor details, such as the number of buttons. The artist then provided an army's distinctive traits with the appropriate colors. Facial features and headwear ultimately distinguished soldiers from one another.

A Russian officer, from the Russian-Japanese war of 1904, bearing his country's standard, bedecked with gold fringing. The infantryman at his side is carrying a rifle. The pair were made by CBG-Mignot at the time of the war.

In 1866, the Prussians beat the Austrians at the Battle of Sadowa in eastern Bohemia. These Austrians— two riflemen, kneeling and standing, and a parading officer— were made by Britains. Note the articulated limbs.

Annamese guards on parade, wearing their famous "salako," a strange woven bamboo hat. Their mold was produced by CBG-Mignot in 1900. Annam was a region of central Vietnam between Tonkin and Cochin China from where French colonial troops were raised, hence the tricolor flag.

The "poilus"—French foot soldiers of the trenches of the First World War—were hindered in battle by their cumbersome backpacks. With typical humor, they dubbed their luggage "The Ace of Diamonds" due to its shape or even "Azor," a dog name equivalent to "Fido," to suggest a hound that follows his master everywhere. These were made by CBG from a mold dating from 1915–20.

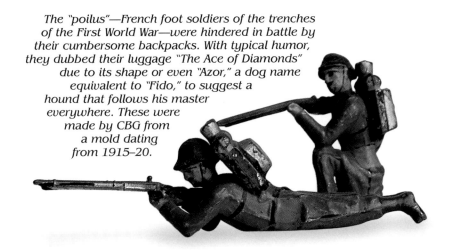

The feeling of action in this mounted
cavalier jumping a hedge is amazing.
It is a lead model manufactured by J.F.
depicting an Algerian or Moroccan
spahi. Both nationalities dressed
in identical ways,
Moroccans generally
wearing blue
and Algerians, red.

This trumpeter, sounding his instrument, is a Prussian from the "white" cuirassiers of the Imperial Guard. The unit was founded by Bismarck after the Battle of Sadowa and existed until the 1914 war. Like the Prussian on the facing page, it is a CBG-Mignot creation from that time.

Another Prussian "white" cuirassier of the Imperial Guard, produced between 1880 and 1890. Note the rifle that the cuirassiers were issued from the nineteenth century onwards.

Under the Ancien Régime in France,
women's hair was used for the
ponytail attached to soldiers'
helmets. It was subsequently
replaced by horsehair.
As well as providing
a certain majestic air,
the ponytail gave extra
protection against saber
blows from the rear. This
dragoon from 1914,
in his greatcoat,
was manufactured
by CBG-Mignot.

These Prussians, from the era when CBG was simply known as Mignot, are heavy cavalrymen from the German army, wearing their famous pointed helmets. While the points on their helmets evoke a certain sense of domination and virility, they were also used to deflect saber blows to the head.

*Hollow lead sailors on parade, from the Third Republic
(1871–1940), were made by J.F., the brand initials
of Le Jouet Fondu. The brand changed its materials
rather than its molds to suit the times, first using lead,
then aluminum, then plastic.*

A soldier from the First World War, lying down.
The X.R. brand from Cosne-sur-Loire in central France
employed only women to produce the hollow-cast
lead figurines that were clearly inspired by those
of CBG-Mignot.

*Russian infantrymen
at work during the
Russian-Japanese war,
produced by
CBG-Mignot (1914). Note
their beret-like hats that
resemble the "polakem"
(or "pokalem") of First
Empire Polish lancers.*

These 1914 French naval fusiliers, made by CBG-Mignot, are also wearing berets, but this time capped with a red pompom. The pompom was fitted to protect sailors from unfortunate knocks to the head walking down ships' low gangways.

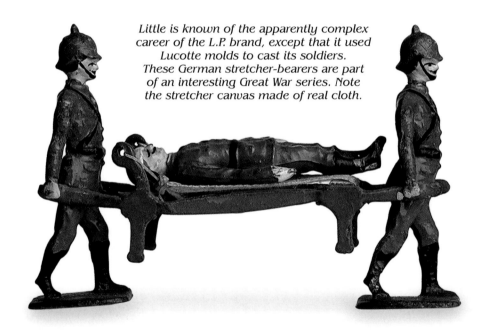

Little is known of the apparently complex career of the L.P. brand, except that it used Lucotte molds to cast its soldiers. These German stretcher-bearers are part of an interesting Great War series. Note the stretcher canvas made of real cloth.

Belgian infantry officer of 1914 charging into battle, made of hollow-cast lead and attributed to the X.R. brand. It is not known for what the initials stand. The brand produced two sizes of soldiers: 2 ⅛ inches and 2 ⅜ inches (55 and 65 mm).

American soldiers in evening wear. With their characteristic sabers, they are no doubt officers. Manufactured by CBG in 1914.

CBG also produced an American Civil War series with Yankees and Confederates in simplified uniforms. The Yankees were painted blue and the Confederates, gray. In reality, uniforms were not so standard and almost every state had its own garb.

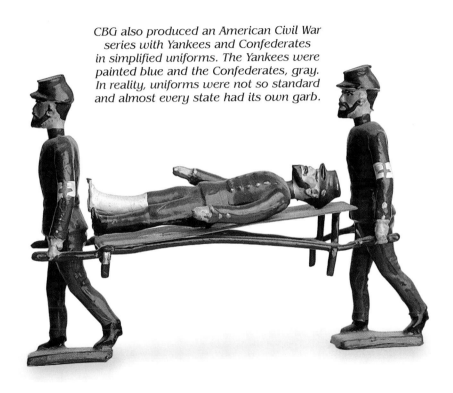

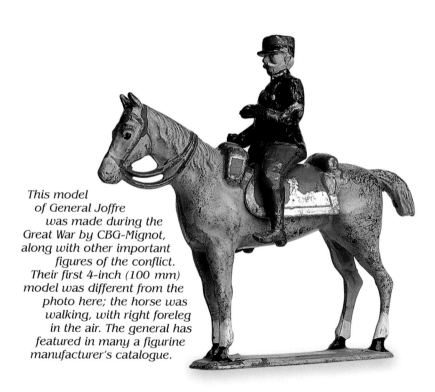

This model
of General Joffre
was made during the
Great War by CBG-Mignot,
along with other important
figures of the conflict.
Their first 4-inch (100 mm)
model was different from the
photo here; the horse was
walking, with right foreleg
in the air. The general has
featured in many a figurine
manufacturer's catalogue.

*The First World War is considered to have been
a "modern" war. Its weaponry is a pet subject of
figurine makers. Here is a CBG-Mignot machine
gunner, wearing an Adrian helmet, in action.
The brand also offered a very realistic ammunition
server with strips of cartridges.*

During the first major worldwide conflict, the bicycle, a recent invention, was used by everyone— Germans, French, and Allies alike. Here is a cyclist wearing a regulation French army cap, issued between 1890 and 1914. The figure was produced by CBG-Mignot at the time and is still available today.

This poilu in his "horizon blue" double-breasted greatcoat is a later model. CBG produced soldiers from all sides in this same pose— charging, one foot on the base, brandishing his weapon.

The miniature sailors, standing to attention on deck, can only watch as their boat disappears. This unusual model of a sinking ship is part of box number 437, entitled "Combat naval devant Port-Arthur" (Naval battle off Port Arthur). Port Arthur is to be found on the tip of the Liaodong Peninsula in China; it has undergone a great many upheavals throughout its history, including the Russian-Japanese War at the start of the twentieth century. On the facing page is a model of a water spurt, also made of lead, depicting a shell explosion at sea—an indispensable element for any child organizing his or her own sea battles.

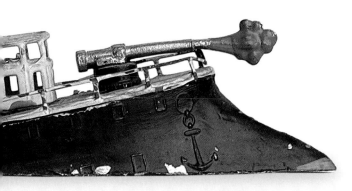

This French dragoon from 1914 equipped with lance, rifle, and revolver was made by Metal Models. It is highly realistic, right down to the beige canvas helmet cover which was used to camouflage the garish, crested, nickel-plated helmet. Note that Metal Models figures are signed on the base by the sculptor Bruno Leibovitz.

Metal Models tin and lead alloy figurines are made for home assembly and painting. This 1916 German army infantry machine gunner, like his neighbor on the facing page, has a canvas helmet cover. Before fitting the cover, the soldier had to unscrew the spike that decorated the top of the helmet.

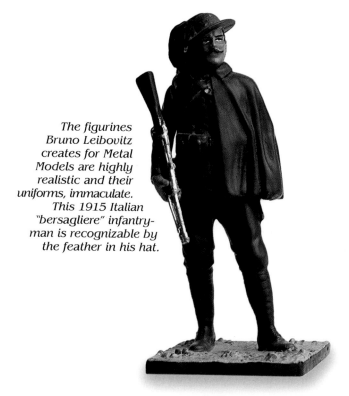

The figurines
Bruno Leibovitz
creates for Metal
Models are highly
realistic and their
uniforms, immaculate.
This 1915 Italian
"bersagliere" infantry-
man is recognizable by
the feather in his hat.

An American army foot soldier from 1917, equipped with a 1903 model Springfield rifle. The American troops arriving in Europe in 1917 were all professional soldiers. By June, there were 1,225,000 of them and by the end of the conflict, three million.

The dromedary is a camel with one hump. The French army used them during their African missions, as seen here with this legionnaire in his blue tunic.

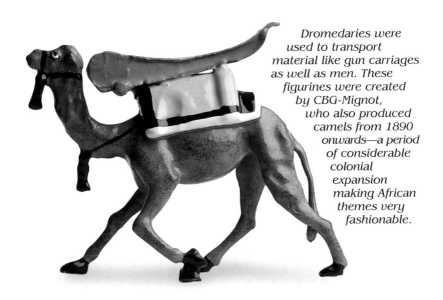

Dromedaries were used to transport material like gun carriages as well as men. These figurines were created by CBG-Mignot, who also produced camels from 1890 onwards—a period of considerable colonial expansion making African themes very fashionable.

A French colonial infantryman from 1930. Such troops were used in Indochina and Black Africa but not North Africa. This soldier, perched on his outsized base, was made by French manufacturers FAEV.

A naval-fusilier from 1914, cast in lead from a plastic figurine mold and painted. This model is from the Mokarex collection, a brand of coffee that gave toy soldiers free with every packet of coffee purchased. Their Great War collection issued forty-seven 2 ⅖-inch (60 mm), solid plastic models.

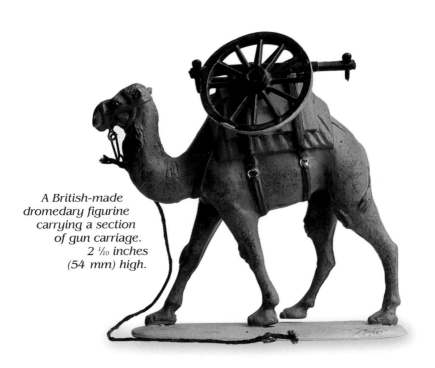

A British-made dromedary figurine carrying a section of gun carriage. 2 ¹/₁₀ inches (54 mm) high.

These French foreign legionnaires from the 1910s were also manufactured in Britain, by H.M. It looks like they are chasing the dromedary on the facing page. Note their canvas neck-flaps, originally improvised by tucking handkerchiefs under their caps to protect against sunstroke.

After much procrastination and hesitation, soldiers of the French army were finally issued with "horizon blue" uniforms and canvas-covered helmets from 1915 onwards. On the right is a stationary bugler; on the left, a foot soldier wearing the first canvas gas mask. . .

The presence of which is a reminder of the one hundred thousand tons of assorted chemical weapons used by both sides during the First World War, responsible for one hundred thousand deaths and one and a half million poisoning victims. These are recent models from antique CBG-Mignot molds.

To assess their range, World War I gunners used telemeters,
geometric land surveying instruments. This small scene
depicts an artillery officer in a uniform from the start
of the war. He is also wearing boots, which
were scarce at this point of the war.
The army's 3,683,000 soldiers suffered a great
boot shortage—many conscripts had to wear
their civilian shoes for several months.

After a trial period, it was decided that the "horizon blue" double-breasted greatcoat was preferable to a blue-gray single-breasted uniform, proffered by belle epoque designer Paul Poiret, as it afforded better protection against the cold. Like the models on the preceding page, these shell carriers are CBG-Mignot figurines.

These German prisoners, surrendering to the Allied forces,
seem instead to be hailing their newfound friends.
CBG-Mignot jumped on the patriotic bandwagon with these
figures, which sold quite well in toyshops during the First World
War and following years. The pointed helmets seen here were
replaced by the end of the war by steel M16 helmets,
resembling the Second World War model.

This trumpeter, wearing his "horizon blue" greatcoat, is a French lancer made by CBG-Mignot. He is wearing his Adrian helmet, which was introduced by Joffre following a ruling of February 21, 1915, to equip the whole army. Three million helmets were issued to poilus in less than a year.

This Prussian cyclist was created by CBG-Mignot, who cast all their bicycles, whether German, French, or British, from the same mold. CBG still produces an excellent British World War II cyclist.

A French soldier from the beginning of the First World War, in red pants and cap. The army phased in a different, more discreet cap in 1915. It was fitted with a "cervellière," a kind of steel shell that protected the skull. The shell only came in three sizes, however—small, medium, and large. Being fairly impractical, it was not widely used.

To provide cover on imaginary battlefields, CBG-Mignot issued these gabions, behind which soldiers could hide to protect themselves against bullets. They were made of woven chestnut wood and contained sand and earth. This type of military protection, like fascines, dates back to Louis XIV's time. In the middle is an infantry officer, armed with his saber, observing the enemy through field glasses.

During the First World War, bicycles played an important role on each side. Adolf Hitler was himself a dispatch runner in the Bavarian army. This is a CBG-Mignot model. The bicycle here is not articulated; the French army, however, used a folding bicycle, invented by its own Captain Gérard.

Prussian infantry soldiers marching. These models were made by CBG-Mignot, from recent molds, in soft pliable lead, which is why the rifles are pointing at different angles.

A Prussian standard-bearer on parade, in his "pickelhaube," or pointed helmet, carrying a saber. To his right is another Prussian, wearing a "pelmütz" or "mütze," a peakless cap worn by the police. On the inside, it had a rosette representing the state and, on the outside, a rosette representing the empire. Manufactured by CBG-Mignot.

A soldier's work is never done. Resting from the battlefield, this French infantry-man on fatigue duty, in red pants and cap, is wearing a white "bourgeron," a short canvas overall also worn by workers in the field.

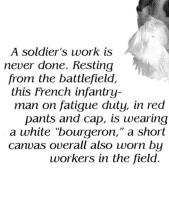

This washing line was also made by CBG-Mignot, another part of their fatigue duty series, lending realism to any scene of childhood fantasy. The reality has less bucolic charm than a child might imagine: the same washing line mold was applicable to either French or German camps; the pants were then painted either blue or green accordingly.

These wounded soldiers are also part of the CBG First World War panorama. Left is an artilleryman with his arm in a sling; right is a nurse from the medical corps carrying a wounded man. The uniforms are those worn at the start of the conflict.

A sister of charity carrying sustenance to the wounded is also an enduring image of the First World War. Made by CBG-Mignot.

Here and facing page, two officers of the French army, produced by Tradition. The first is decorated with the same medals and wearing the same uniform as a certain Charles Péguy, also a cavalry officer, who was killed at the Battle of the Marne at Plessis-L'Evèque, just outside Paris, in September 1914.

This second French officer is a legionnaire from the beginning of the twentieth century. Note the field glasses and rolled blanket, slung across his chest. For officers at the time, mustaches were de rigueur.

This foreign legion drummer has tent poles in his backpack. Tents could accommodate several soldiers, so each orderly would carry part of the equipment. Manufactured recently by Tradition.

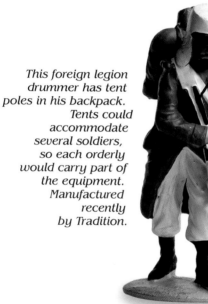

North African infantrymen played "nouba" music. These two musicians are being led by a ram, the traditional regimental mascot. During the Crimean War, the Algerian or Moroccan infantry corps became known as "turcos," due to their uniforms that the Russians confused with those of Turkish soldiers.

This World War I
Moroccan infantryman,
scanning the horizon,
is a lead cast from a
Mokarex figurine mold
(see pages 113 and 215).
He is wearing a fez—
a truncated wool
hat—traditional
headwear in some
North African countries.
Note the helmet attached
to his belt on the left.

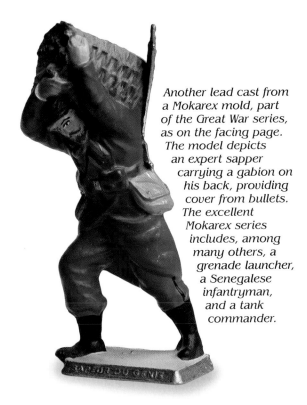

Another lead cast from a Mokarex mold, part of the Great War series, as on the facing page. The model depicts an expert sapper carrying a gabion on his back, providing cover from bullets. The excellent Mokarex series includes, among many others, a grenade launcher, a Senegalese infantryman, and a tank commander.

At the beginning, the French spahis were a Turkish cavalry brigade, called "sipahis." The brigade, created in 1834, was mainly composed of Turkish nationals in French service, particularly in Syria between 1919 and 1942. The figurine is made by the Spanish brand Alymer, a manufacturer of toy soldiers since the end of the 1950s.

This realistic tripod-fitted Hotchkiss machine gun, manned by a legionnaire, is a popular CBG-Mignot model from 1914. Other manufacturers, like X.R., have produced similar figurines but with a standard machine gun to depict artillerymen from other nations in the conflict.

During the 1930s, the G.M. brand (Georges Munckle) produced this mounted courier in hollow-cast lead. His machine is a French-made Terrot, the first company in Europe to manufacture motorcycles, located in Dijon. What is gained in excitement with the shooting pose is lost in realism.

This camel, bearing parts of a field cannon, is made by Heyde, a German manufacturer. The company was founded at the end of the nineteenth century in Dresden by Georg Heyde but did not survive World War II. Heyde was the equivalent in Germany of CBG-Mignot in France in terms of popularity.

In his own inimitable style, the craftsman Jean-Pierre Feigly still produces traditional lead soldiers today, such as these two English privates, wearing their legendary, so-called "shaving-dish" helmets.

Another pair of soldiers standing to attention, as on the facing page. This duo was made by Tradition and featured in the British campaign in Sudan. Sudan's name derives from the Arabic phrase "bilad as-sudan" meaning "land of the blacks." Their belts are fitted with the traditional British army buckle.

No need to introduce this figure—Leonard Spencer Churchill, the British prime minister from 1940–45 and 1951–55. Other major historical players have also been sculpted in lead miniature form such as De Gaulle, Mussolini, and Hitler. This is a hollow-cast lead model, created by L.R., the model manufacturer Louis Roussy.

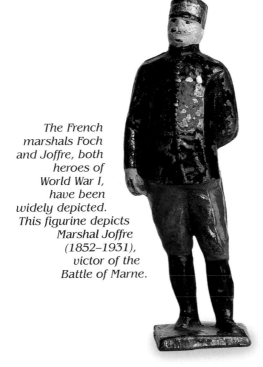

The French marshals Foch and Joffre, both heroes of World War I, have been widely depicted. This figurine depicts Marshal Joffre (1852–1931), victor of the Battle of Marne.

During World War II, the Germans raised troops in India. This soldier was cast in a Tradition mold and painted by the artist Guilien.

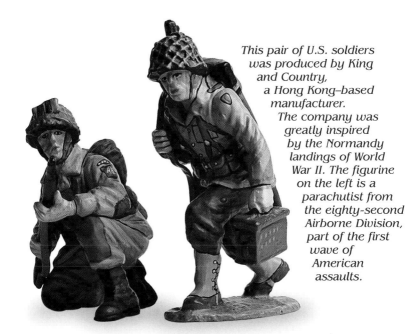

This pair of U.S. soldiers was produced by King and Country, a Hong Kong–based manufacturer. The company was greatly inspired by the Normandy landings of World War II. The figurine on the left is a parachutist from the eighty-second Airborne Division, part of the first wave of American assaults.

CBG-Mignot has issued more recent subjects, such as these French naval musicians from the 1950s. Despite the ascendancy of plastic in figurine production, CBG-Mignot maintained its predominance in the lead soldier market, a position it has held for over a century. Whole battalions of toy soldiers, in tight formation, used to stream out of CBG factories.

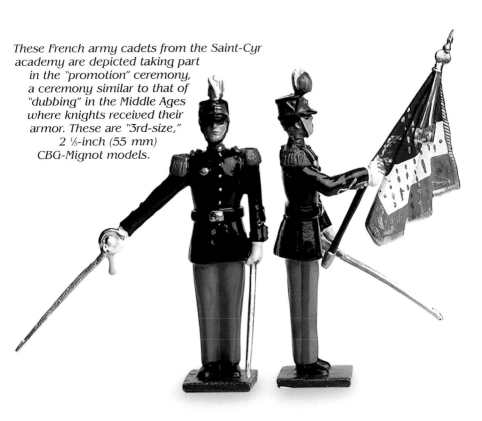

These French army cadets from the Saint-Cyr academy are depicted taking part in the "promotion" ceremony, a ceremony similar to that of "dubbing" in the Middle Ages where knights received their armor. These are "3rd-size," 2 ⅕-inch (55 mm) CBG-Mignot models.

At the French Bastille Day parade on July 14, the French foreign legion receives the loudest cheers. Their popularity has led to wide-scale production by nearly all manufacturers. These models depict today's legionnaires on large bases of paving stones.

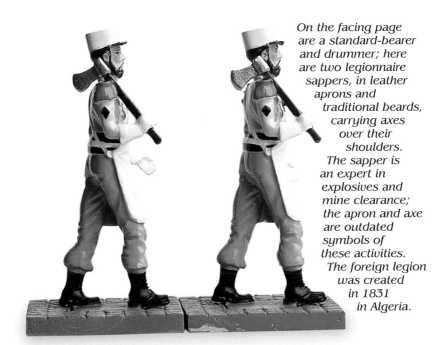

On the facing page are a standard-bearer and drummer; here are two legionnaire sappers, in leather aprons and traditional beards, carrying axes over their shoulders. The sapper is an expert in explosives and mine clearance; the apron and axe are outdated symbols of these activities. The foreign legion was created in 1831 in Algeria.

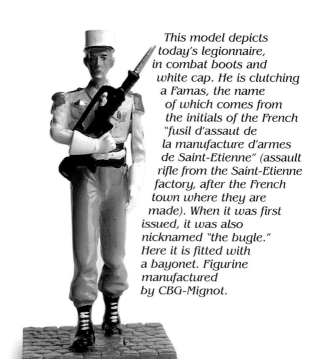

This model depicts today's legionnaire, in combat boots and white cap. He is clutching a Famas, the name of which comes from the initials of the French "fusil d'assaut de la manufacture d'armes de Saint-Etienne" (assault rifle from the Saint-Etienne factory, after the French town where they are made). When it was first issued, it was also nicknamed "the bugle." Here it is fitted with a bayonet. Figurine manufactured by CBG-Mignot.

In the French army, parachutists in combat uniform are a prestigious unit. They are known as "red berets"; "green berets," meanwhile, are foreign legion parachutists.
This pair of paras was made by Hispania, a Spanish manufacturer of figurines.

III

ALUMINUM
toy soldiers

L ead is heavy; it bends and it breaks. When Emile Quirin had the idea, at the beginning of the 1930s, to mold toy soldiers in aluminum— a light and miraculously flexible alloy—toy vendors, to a man, adopted his product. The main advantage of aluminum is that it is practically unbreakable, unlike lead. Simply take a look at a box of aluminum soldiers from more than fifty years ago. Several generations of children will have played with it but only the tips of cowboys' pistols, soldiers' rifles, or Indians' arrows will have suffered the rigors of children's imaginations— and a broken arrow or a muzzle-less gun has never stopped a child from having fun.

Between 1938 and 1940, Quiralu, like so many other manufacturers in the past and present, traveled back in time to produce this readily identifiable, almost caricatural Napoleon I. The same brand made another, almost identical Napoleon on horseback, again with his hand tucked away; however, all four feet of the steed are on the ground, with no base.

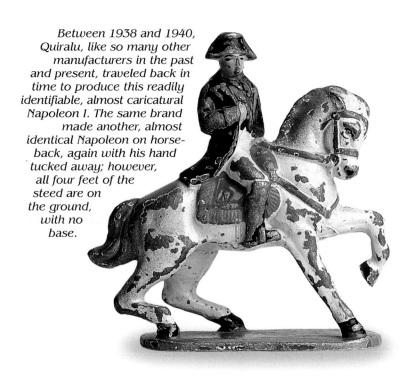

This pair of light infantry grenadiers of the Imperial Guard presenting arms are from the same period as the figurine on the facing page. They are also Quiralu productions on round bases.

Quiralu has
produced a great
many horses, with different
degrees of workmanship.
The company has had
a distinguished range
of craftsmen over the
years whose names
unfortunately have
been lost to history.
Here is a spahi,
identifiable by his fez.

Here is another mounted spahi, produced between 1933 and 1940 by Quiralu. The company issued a third model bearing a trumpet attached to his back by a thin metal wire.

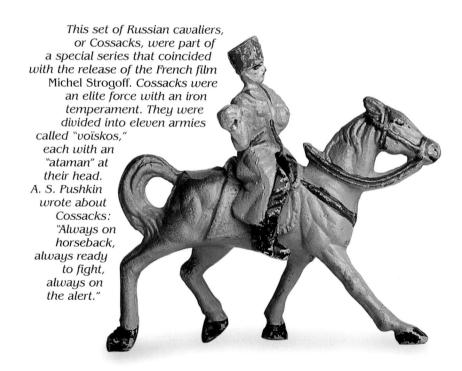

This set of Russian cavaliers, or Cossacks, were part of a special series that coincided with the release of the French film Michel Strogoff. Cossacks were an elite force with an iron temperament. They were divided into eleven armies called "voïskos," each with an "ataman" at their head. A. S. Pushkin wrote about Cossacks: "Always on horseback, always ready to fight, always on the alert."

Quiralu has made numerous
models of the French
Republican Guard, on foot
as well as horseback.
Its regimental band featured
fifteen different instruments,
including trumpeters, drummers,
and cymbalists.
This rider and
steed are in fact
mismatched,
as the horse
belongs to
a cadet.

This is the Quiralu version of the foreign legion, equipped with neck-flaps. This parade-ground version appeared in 1933 and was produced until 1940. The brand issued other legionnaire drummers with hands in a different position.

These Moroccan infantrymen, rifles over shoulders, with ballooning white pants and blue tunics, were also made by Quiralu. Another version came in khaki jacket and pants. Circa 1933–40.

This lithe engineer fixing telephone cables is a member of the Signal Corps, produced by Quiralu in the 1930s. The telegraph pole is made of wood and marketed by Boislux, who issued other wooden accessories such as Maginot Line defense units, ruined walls, and a canteen shelter. On the left is an aluminum fir tree for an authentic eastern French setting.

These 1 ⁹/₁₀-inch (47 mm)-high caricatures of firefighters, made by Quiralu, were designed for younger children. With their plump bellies and comic helmets, they are the firefighters of children's tales. The box set was entitled "Pompiers de Nanterre" (Nanterre Firefighters), after the town outside Paris. The design on the cover featured precise details of its restaurants and town hall.

Parading British soldiers from 1939. An American officer, Anson Mills, dreamed up the modern combat uniform in 1877. Great Britain was the first nation to adopt his version.

Two navy buglers on parade. These two French sailors, like the privates on the facing page, are Quiralu models produced during the 1933–40 period.

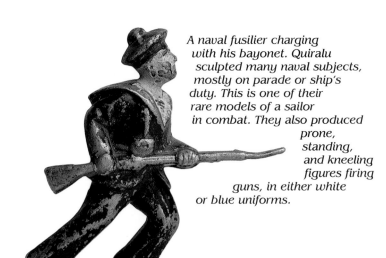

A naval fusilier charging with his bayonet. Quiralu sculpted many naval subjects, mostly on parade or ship's duty. This is one of their rare models of a sailor in combat. They also produced prone, standing, and kneeling figures firing guns, in either white or blue uniforms.

Scottish Highlanders wearing their famous carded and pleated wool kilt. In the field, they would protect their kilts with beige canvas aprons. These two bagpipe players were produced by Quiralu.

Being a chef in the Great War was no picnic. Guy Devautour, a specialist in military matters, reminds us that military chefs were unsung heroes of the conflict. They would risk their lives on a daily basis, in unenviable conditions, to provide food for the soldiers at the front. Furthermore, if the soup was ever cold when it reached its destination, it was the chef's turn for a mouthful. Produced by Quiralu in the 1930s.

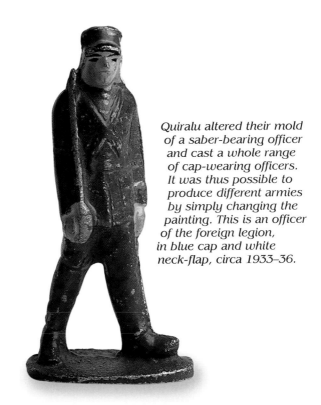

Quiralu altered their mold
of a saber-bearing officer
and cast a whole range
of cap-wearing officers.
It was thus possible to
produce different armies
by simply changing the
painting. This is an officer
of the foreign legion,
in blue cap and white
neck-flap, circa 1933–36.

From 1938, Quiralu produced dromedary riders with a base. Then, between 1955 and 1960, they re-released the "Moghazni" dromedary-rider series in homage to the Saharan force created by General Laperrine, the hero of Fort Saganne.

Quiralu inspired other manufacturers, as with this dromedary-mounted officer made by Bicail and Ganivet, a Tunisian toy brand.

*It was possible to add extra pairs of draft horses
to this horse-drawn gun carriage. It was made
by Quiralu, circa 1933–40.
Their attention to sculpture and
casting is impeccable.
The original set included
three pairs of horses, with
and without riders, . . .*

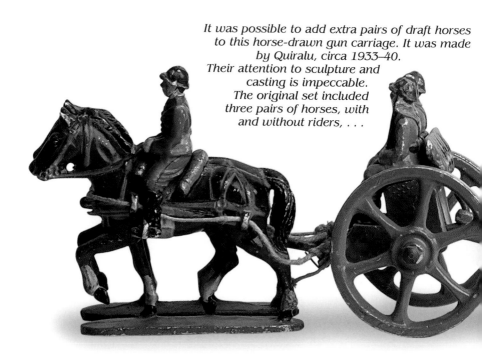

*. . . a front-axle unit with three seated gunners,
and a 3-inch (75 mm) field gun in tow. Another set
featured a horse-drawn ammunition trailer.
The soldiers' uniforms were available
in "horizon blue" or khaki,
according to children's tastes
between the two wars.*

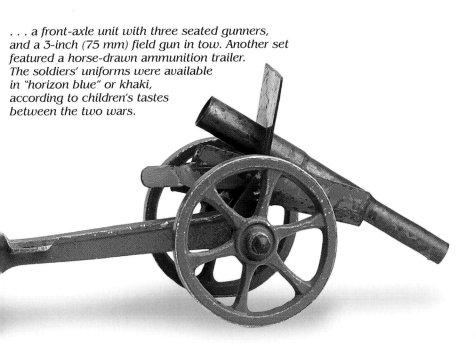

These Zouaves on parade, their weapons perched on their right shoulders, were produced by Quiralu at the end of the 1930s.

*Zouaves on parade,
puffing into their
bugles, producing
a music only
children can hear.*

Quiralu dreamed up almost everything.
This foot soldier, in Adrian helmet and puttees,
is pushing an aluminum wheelbarrow
loaded with an ammunition crate.
This model, like those on the facing page,
is part of the fatigue duty series.
Circa 1933–40.

These soldiers on fatigue duty, in puttees and forage caps, are lugging their mess tins. Note the haversack on their backs. The various fatigue duty activities were well represented by Quiralu, in all their splendor, and even featured a full field kitchen with soldiers peling potatoes— the most noble of chores.

*Quiralu created a
number of figurines of
infantrymen in combat,
such as these prone
and kneeling gunmen,
each on its own base.
Circa 1933–40.*

*This machine gunner, with his Hotchkiss,
had an additional ammunition supplier
feeding strips of cartridges.*

In their white summer uniforms, guns on their shoulders and bayonets in their belts, these figurines depict sailors on parade. Quiralu used a similar mold to produce naval fusiliers, identifiable by their gaiters.

A naval officer, this time, saber in hand, parading in his summer uniform. Also manufactured by Quiralu.

This impressive wounded soldier is part of Quiralu's medical corps series. Like all wounded soldiers, he has his arm in a sling and a bandage around his head. He is, however, still strong enough to stand. Alongside are two dogs, also made of aluminum, which featured in other series, such as the farmyard range. Circa 1933–40.

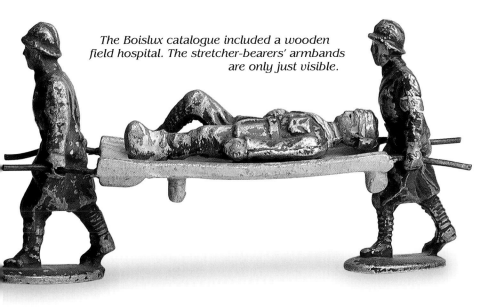

The Boislux catalogue included a wooden field hospital. The stretcher-bearers' armbands are only just visible.

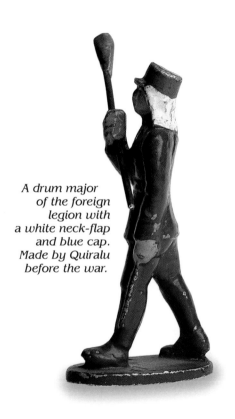

A drum major
of the foreign
legion with
a white neck-flap
and blue cap.
Made by Quiralu
before the war.

This dispatch rider cast in one block, complete with Adrian helmet and rifle slung over his shoulder, was available in blue and khaki. The motorbike is a Terrot model with parallelogram forks and gas tank in the seat.

It would be good to know who designed this superb 1930 Quiralu horse, with its brushed-back ears and its self-satisfied stride. The rider, a general staff officer in a cap, also has a certain class. Quiralu produced a similar model, no doubt by the same designer: its tail is half-length and the rider, a general, is wearing a cocked hat.

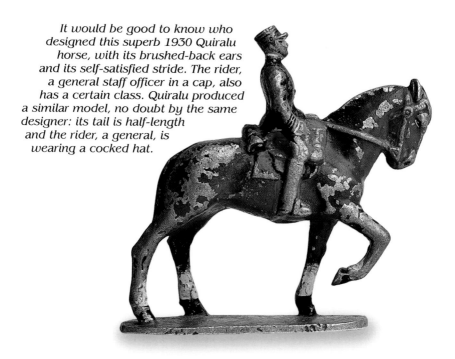

This mounted dragoon, dressed in an overcoat and carrying his gun over his shoulder, was available in "horizon blue" or khaki. Just such a field soldier would subsequently feature in the "phony war," before joining the great exodus of refugees who fled the north of France. Quiralu, 1933–40.

Quiralu also paid homage to Alpine chasseurs, with their large flat caps pulled over their heads. This model is a muleteer, part of a convoy carrying a mountain gun; another mule bears the carriage. Notice the small hole in the mouth of the mule, through which to pass a short length of cord for the chasseur to guide the horse over difficult terrain.

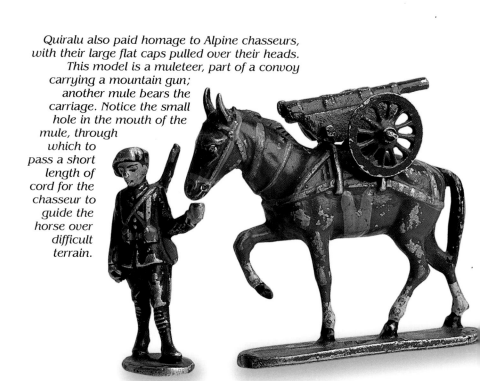

Kit-carrying mule accompanying all types of soldiers. It also has a hole through which to thread its reins. Made by Quiralu in the prewar period.

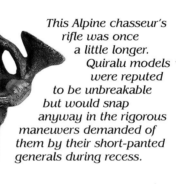

This Alpine chasseur's
rifle was once
a little longer.
Quiralu models
were reputed
to be unbreakable
but would snap
anyway in the rigorous
maneuvers demanded of
them by their short-panted
generals during recess.

This pair of Alpine chasseurs, busy with their machine gun, are of the same brand and era as the soldier on the facing page. The character on his knees with a box under his arm is a fellow gunner providing ammunition.

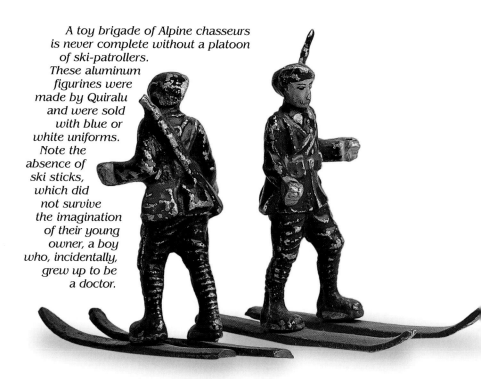

A toy brigade of Alpine chasseurs is never complete without a platoon of ski-patrollers. These aluminum figurines were made by Quiralu and were sold with blue or white uniforms. Note the absence of ski sticks, which did not survive the imagination of their young owner, a boy who, incidentally, grew up to be a doctor.

Spurred on by its success, Quiralu was able to sculpt every aspect of the army, including the air force, such as this officer and trooper, rifle slung over shoulder. The company issued two series of pilots on parade, the first during the 1930s; the second in the 1950s. Furthermore, in 1952, Quiralu produced pilots in flying regalia, with gas mask, backpack parachute, and brown leather headband, as well as a number of airplanes.

It is not hard to imagine this rebel Arab,
in the half-light of dawn, weaving
his way through the dunes, knife
in one hand, rifle in the other.
It was produced by G.M. (George
Munckle), a manufacturer of
hollow-cast lead models,
who started using
aluminum in 1936
under the Gemalux
brand name.

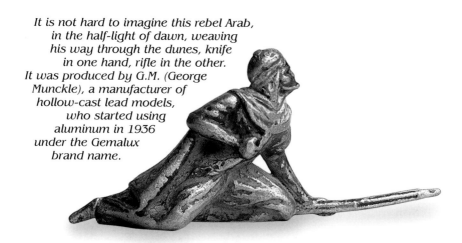

An Indian chasseur from the English army, wearing his trademark turban. This aluminum model is not made by Quiralu but by Gemalux, who produced models of the English, Russian, and Ethiopian armies, among others.

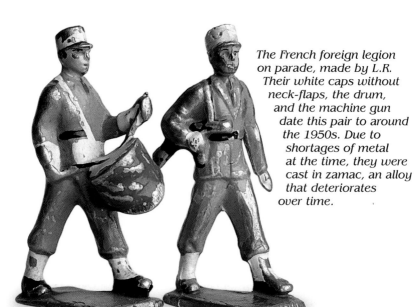

The French foreign legion on parade, made by L.R. Their white caps without neck-flaps, the drum, and the machine gun date this pair to around the 1950s. Due to shortages of metal at the time, they were cast in zamac, an alloy that deteriorates over time.

*The legendary sapper, with axe over his shoulder
and leather apron, would be incomplete without his long
beard. Alongside him, two foreign legion buglers.
The three figures were produced by Bicail
and Ganivet, in Tunisia.*

From 1945 to 1950, Mignalu produced a series of large-scale 4 ³⁄₁₀-inch (110 mm)-high aluminum soldiers called the Mignalu 1500, which depicted different armies of the era. These sailors on parade, rifles on shoulders, were accompanied by a drummer, an Alpine chasseur, Monaco Guards, and a cadet.

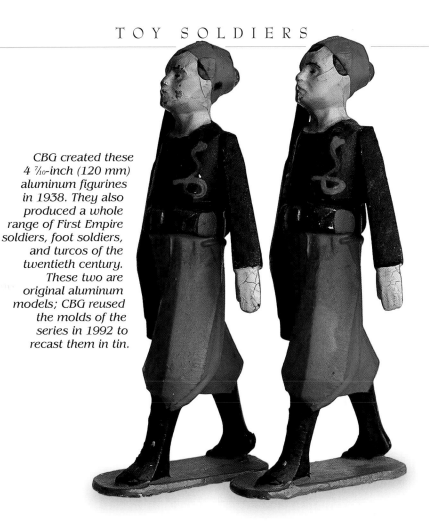

CBG created these 4 7/10-inch (120 mm) aluminum figurines in 1938. They also produced a whole range of First Empire soldiers, foot soldiers, and turcos of the twentieth century. These two are original aluminum models; CBG reused the molds of the series in 1992 to recast them in tin.

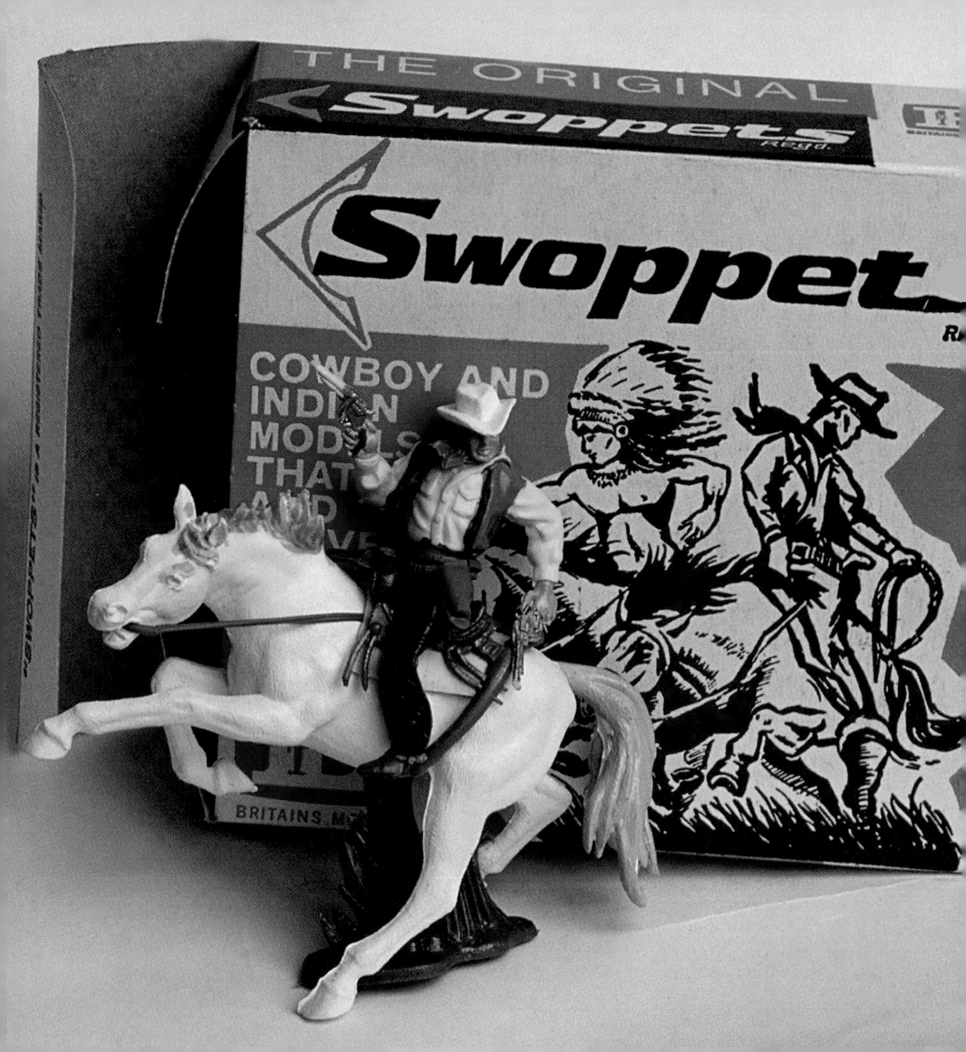

THE ORIGINAL
Swoppets
Regd.
Swoppet
COWBOY AND
BRITAINS

IV

PLASTIC
toy soldiers

T he soldiers in this last chapter are not exclusively made of plastic. Indeed, since the silver "gargoyles" of the Middle Ages (see page 17), creators have searched continuously to find materials that are easy to work, as light as possible, and made with inexpensive primary materials. With their switch from silver to lead—first solid then hollow-cast—then to aluminum, toy soldier manufacturers were on the right track. You will find here examples of different attempts to produce "composition" figurines from materials other than metal, in particular using unusual products like glue, kaolin, flour, and plaster.

The best-known plastic toy soldier brand in Europe is Starlux, which was created before World War II by the craftsman Elie Tarroux. His son-in-law, Pierre Beffara, introduced Starlux to its major successes in the 1950s and 1960s. This model of a gallant knight, brandishing his mace, was a relatively late arrival to the Starlux catalogue— part of their 1958 medieval series, which opened with knights on foot or horseback.

Starlux knights were detachable and could be sold on different horses. Such is the case with the pair of identical knights on these pages. Note the eagle stenciled on the horse's housing. The shape of the base dates this model to 1965.

Among Starlux's most sought-after figurines is this ivory plastic model. Most of the brand's production was designed by Laurent Texidor, including this knight, or Maurice Massat— both official Starlux sculptors.

Mounted horses
from the dark
ages were
sold wearing
harnesses
(facing page),
housing (page 307),
or caparisons.
This model was
first sold in 1962
and still featured
in Starlux's
catalogue of 1971.
It cost the equivalent
of a mere fifty cents.

This small regimental standard-bearer from the Ancien Régime would have been the perfect prize for a boy with good grades—providing him with the motivation he needed to study his history lessons while setting his imagination whirring.

*Like the standard-bearer
on the facing page, this model was
designed by Pierre de Bièville,
founder of Segom, a French brand
that pioneered the use of plastic
in toy soldier production.
Segom manufactured
both painted and
unpainted figurines.*

These are First Empire soldiers,
manufactured by MDM and designed by
a former CBG-Mignot
craftsman,
René Daniel,
who created
his own brand
in 1955.
He specialized in
the First Empire,
producing this
superb Napoleon
and his Dutch
grenadiers.
Napoleon's
brother, Louis,
was king of
Holland.

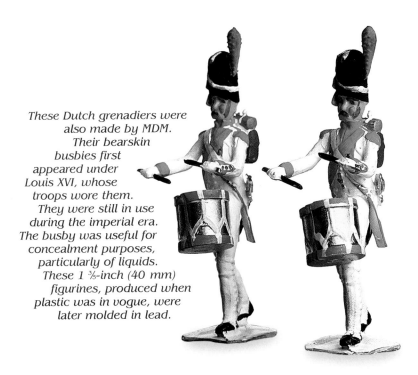

These Dutch grenadiers were also made by MDM. Their bearskin busbies first appeared under Louis XVI, whose troops wore them. They were still in use during the imperial era. The busby was useful for concealment purposes, particularly of liquids. These 1 ⅗-inch (40 mm) figurines, produced when plastic was in vogue, were later molded in lead.

Dragoon officer of the twenty-fourth regiment of the Imperial Guard. In the Starlux catalogue, its reference is FH 60620. Collector Christian Blondeau, in his book (see page 379), notes that from 1964 to the present day, Starlux has produced 259 standing pieces and 125 models on horseback from the First Empire.

*Emperor Napoleon's per-
sonal manservant was a
Mameluke by the name of
Roustan, or Roustam,
who also featured in
the Starlux range.
Roustam was
born in Georgia
in 1780 and died
in Dourdan, near
Paris, in 1850.
He was a gift
to Napoleon I
from the sheik
of Cairo.*

In French toy soldier legend, the Alexandres should not be confused—first there is Pierre Alexandre, an artist from 1930–50, who has no relation to his contemporary, Alexandre Ballada. However, it was a third, Claude Alexandre, who produced these figurines. He set his creations using resin—in this case, an 1812 carabineer charging.

A dragoon cymbalist of the Imperial Guard in resin, by Claude Alexandre. Like most contemporary figurine makers, he sculpts using a lead alloy called "white metal" to produce a 2 ⅖-inch (70 mm) mold. In the industry, Starlux included, sculptures are made large scale, 7–8 inches (18–20 cm) high, then reduced by pantography.

A Berg Chevau-Léger lancer, made by Starlux. In the manufacturer's catalogue, the piece does not exist in this format. Le Royaume, a company that also produces miniatures, supplied detachable accessories, like this lance.

These Starlux models were produced while the distinguished figurine sculptor Texidor was still working with the company. They are very rare, being among the company's last efforts to compete on the historical figurine market. They are 2 ¹/₁₀-inch (54 mm)-high First Empire soldiers that are also unusual because one has a bugle, an instrument that did not exist at the time.

It is not easy to give a date or origin to this composition figurine. All we know is that it came from Germany.

*This Native American Indian
is also a composition piece,
made of plaster, flour,
whiting, and glue.
It dates from the 1940s,
a period when primary
materials were limited.*

The Astrid brand possibly never released a model soldier with a base. On this page is a Native American warrior, tomahawk in hand; facing page, a gun-toting cowboy.

At the start of the 1960s, Astrid used polystyrene to make their figurines. The models did not sit comfortably side-by-side with other brands as they were too big. Two series existed: 3-inch and 3 ³/₁₀-inch (80 and 85 mm) models.

This model, dubbed "The Rodeo Cowboy," was produced in Starlux's early days (1953) and measures 3 inches (75 mm) from the tip of the front right leg to the cowboy's eyes. The horse could be fitted with a cowboy in different postures: with or without a lasso, or firing a gun.

Starlux cowboys from the start of the plastic period are easily identifiable by their solid, slightly plump appearance and by their colored materials. This cavalryman measures 2 ½ inches (64 mm) high. With Starlux, the larger a model was, the more elegant its contours became; in this way the toy became the figurine.

This trapper in his famous fringed jacket is, of course, Davy Crockett. It was manufactured by Jim, in 1957, after gaining Walt Disney Productions' permission, a detail that features on the base by the brand name.

A Native American Sioux by Jim, a brand created in 1950. Their first models were molded in yellow or red acetate, ideal colors for "redskins." Jim's Farwest series, produced between 1950 and 1965, included thirty-eight Native Americans.

These exquisite 2 ½-inch (64 mm) models are made by Elastolin. The company eventually abandoned the past and replaced its trademark kaolin and sawdust materials for modern plastic.

The standing character is Winnetou, from a novel by Karl May. He was the hero of a number of films during the 1950s. Note the detail on the faces of Elastolin figurines from this period, in particular the face of the Sioux chief smoking his peace pipe.

A French soldier from the First Empire produced by Britains. Modern figurines from this brand are easily identifiable by their green aluminum base on which the brand name is written.

An English soldier manufactured by Britains. This particular brand of plastic figurine was very popular and sold around the world.

The Bon-Dufour brand was founded in 1890. They were reputed to be unbreakable and were molded from a mixture of ingredients like plaster, flour, papier mâché, and sawdust.

These 3 ⁷/₁₀-inch (95 mm) cuirassiers on foot were part of a twelve-piece boxed set which included a bandy-legged cavalier and a horse. Note the absence of bases on these models (here and facing page) to make them look more like children's toys.

Bon-Dufour also made this soldier on parade. Many manufacturers around Europe, like Fontanini in Italy, Cellose in France, and Strola in Germany, produced models in this style that need very little attention to detail.

French Second Empire carabineers of the guard from 1870, sold by Giroux in Paris. It is probable that they were imported from Sonneberg in Germany, who supplied Giroux with numerous figurines.

The Giroux establishment was created in 1799 on rue du Coq Saint Honoré in Paris, before being rehoused on rue de Marengo, near the Louvre. It is said it was one of the most elegant boutiques in Paris. In light of the models it sold, it is easy to believe.

These two delightful Zouaves, viewed front and back, show the finesse of design and beauty in movement that make them real window display items. The Giroux establishment (see also page 336) probably disappeared at the end of the nineteenth century.

Lead, plastic, or aluminum soldier manufacturers would switch primary materials according to whim and current trends. These caricature soldiers were first made in aluminum by Quiralu in the 1930s to 1950s, then reproduced in plastic in the 1960s.

This friendly looking plastic soldier on his rocking horse was made for infants by Quiralu. It is more evocative of fairy tales than the harsh realities of the battlefield.

The Britains company, founded in 1893, has left its
mark on the history of toy soldiers in many ways.
As concerns their plastic soldier output, in 1959
they produced "Swoppets," miniatures with
interchangeable equipment. Here are the Gordon
Highlanders—a Scottish regiment from the Details
series—who became famous at Waterloo.

Britains drew heavily on the American Civil War. They had great commercial success, in 1963, when they commemorated the centenary of the conflict. From more exotic climes, the Sudanese warrior is highly realistic—as is the Confederate loading his rifle.

A spahi officer
in a burnous, with
field glasses, by J.R.D.
These figurines were
fashioned in a material
composed of powdered
slate, which made them
hard and heavy.

*These remarkable
dismounted dromedary
riders are the unusual height
of 3 ³⁄₁₀ inches (85 mm).
They were produced in 1931
for the colonial exhibition.
The first series of J.R.D.
soldiers dealt exclusively
with colonial troops;
other military figurines
followed afterwards.*

This kneeling rifleman, by the D.C. brand, is molded from flour and plaster, cheap materials essentially used during shortages. In the postwar years, figurines made of this material proliferated, while producers awaited better days . . .

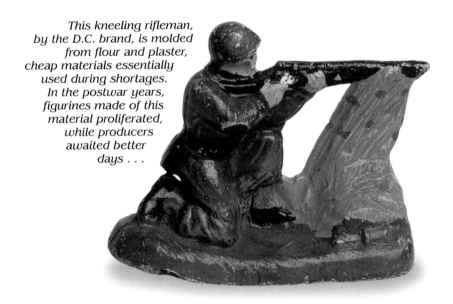

. . . and the arrival of plastic soldiers. Plastic brought with it detail and realism but lost some of the poetry. Toureg soldiers standing to attention, by D.C. (Domage et Cie).

A motorcyclist from
the 1930s, during the period
when the army used Terrot and
Gnome et Rhône motorbikes.
This machine is neither, but
possibly a hybrid of
the two. Made by D.C.

Horses were still very present in the French army at the end of the 1930s, which is when this cavalier was probably produced, using whiting. Whiting was used in the immediate postwar period by Elie Tarroux, the founder of Starlux.

A very attractive model of a legionnaire charging, with his neck-flap waving in the wind. The D.C. company also produced Alpine chasseurs, Zouaves, dromedary riders, sailors, and soldiers from the sultan of Morocco's guard.

Figurine specialist François Beaumont dates this spahi from just after the war. It is composed of a material made by the company Inca France.

Produced exclusively for the store La Boîte de Soldats, this 1939 foot soldier is made of resin. It measures 2 ⅘ inches (70 mm) and was first sculpted larger-scale in boxwood by Pierre Flamen, a retired soldier. The detail on the MAS 36 rifle and equipment is striking.

Sporting leggings and with field glasses around his neck, this infantry lieutenant is directing his troops. Only thirty copies of each soldier in this series were produced. There were eleven different models, all from the same period. Marked with the F.B. brand under the base.

The German brand Elastolin issued catalogues full of Third Reich toy soldiers. These musicians feature in the 1937 catalogue under the reference "0/47/2, Pfeifer" (piper), priced at 0.25 Deutsch marks. Elastolin was a material composed of sawdust, kaolin, and glue.

The Muller and Freyer brand made a name for itself with its Elastolin modeling product, as described facing page. The company achieved such rapid and great success with this material that they adopted it as its brand name.

This 2 ⅔-inch (70 mm)-high
Luftwaffe pilot was produced in
1936 by Lineol. The brand is marked
on the base. Next to him
is a Finnish grenadier
in winter uniform,
circa 1939.

Lineol also made composition French soldiers, like this 2 ⅖-inch (60 mm) mounted spahi, dating from 1932.

*Colonialization and subsequent local resistance
inspired toy soldier manufacturers, who produced
a number of colonial soldiers in law and order roles.*

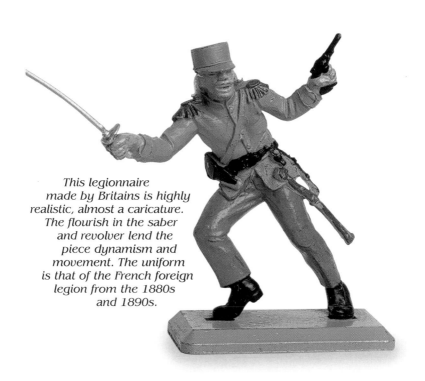

This legionnaire made by Britains is highly realistic, almost a caricature. The flourish in the saber and revolver lend the piece dynamism and movement. The uniform is that of the French foreign legion from the 1880s and 1890s.

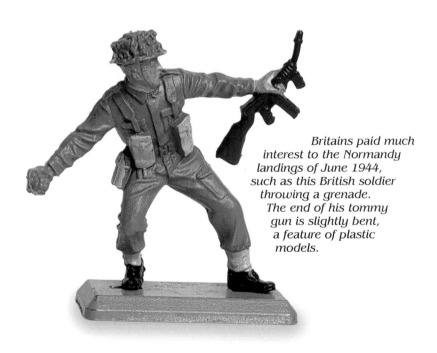

Britains paid much interest to the Normandy landings of June 1944, such as this British soldier throwing a grenade. The end of his tommy gun is slightly bent, a feature of plastic models.

To illustrate the June 6 landing, Britains produced these American soldiers in the heat of battle with their USM rifles.

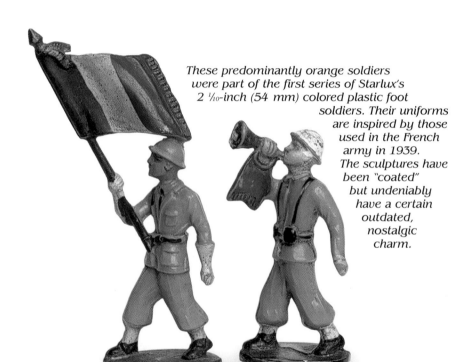

These predominantly orange soldiers were part of the first series of Starlux's 2 ¹/₁₀-inch (54 mm) colored plastic foot soldiers. Their uniforms are inspired by those used in the French army in 1939. The sculptures have been "coated" but undeniably have a certain outdated, nostalgic charm.

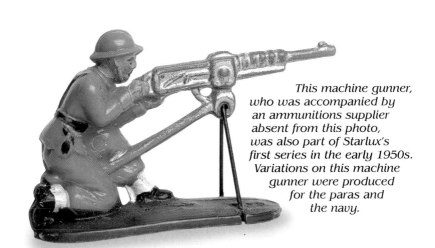

This machine gunner, who was accompanied by an ammunitions supplier absent from this photo, was also part of Starlux's first series in the early 1950s. Variations on this machine gunner were produced for the paras and the navy.

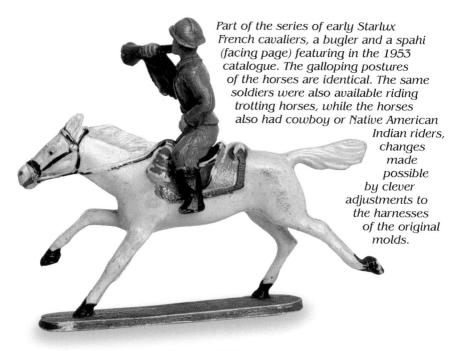

Part of the series of early Starlux French cavaliers, a bugler and a spahi (facing page) featuring in the 1953 catalogue. The galloping postures of the horses are identical. The same soldiers were also available riding trotting horses, while the horses also had cowboy or Native American Indian riders, changes made possible by clever adjustments to the harnesses of the original molds.

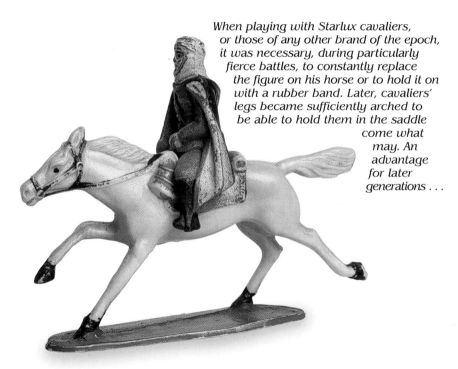

*When playing with Starlux cavaliers,
or those of any other brand of the epoch,
it was necessary, during particularly
fierce battles, to constantly replace
the figure on his horse or to hold it on
with a rubber band. Later, cavaliers'
legs became sufficiently arched to
be able to hold them in the saddle
come what
may. An
advantage
for later
generations . . .*

These Starlux soldiers, with their rectangular bases and keen profiles, are from the 1970s. They are to be found in the brand's catalogues under the reference LM, standing for legion and music. Part of a deluxe series.

These are later models of German World War II soldiers, designed by Maurice Massat in 1972. They appeared in the Starlux catalogue the following year. The arms were molded then attached separately. The various elements can be combined in numerous poses.

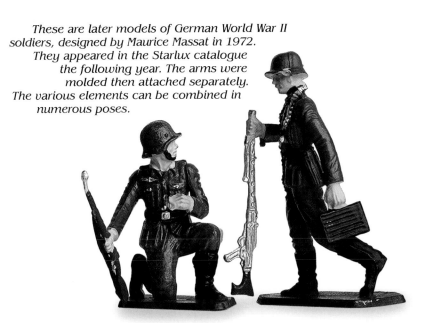

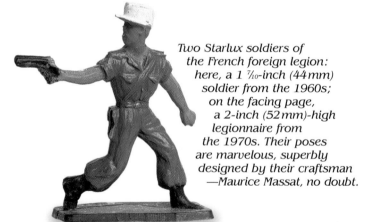

Two Starlux soldiers of
the French foreign legion:
here, a 1 7/10-inch (44mm)
soldier from the 1960s;
on the facing page,
a 2-inch (52mm)-high
legionnaire from
the 1970s. Their poses
are marvelous, superbly
designed by their craftsman
—Maurice Massat, no doubt.

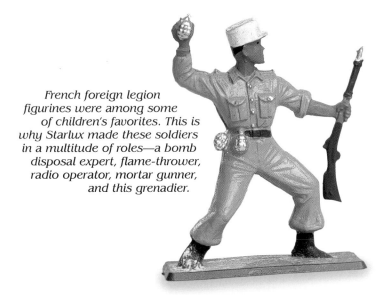

French foreign legion figurines were among some of children's favorites. This is why Starlux made these soldiers in a multitude of roles—a bomb disposal expert, flame-thrower, radio operator, mortar gunner, and this grenadier.

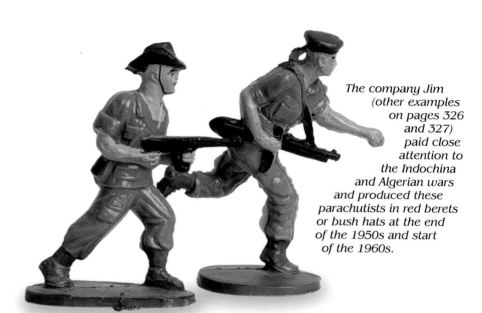

The company Jim (other examples on pages 326 and 327) paid close attention to the Indochina and Algerian wars and produced these parachutists in red berets or bush hats at the end of the 1950s and start of the 1960s.

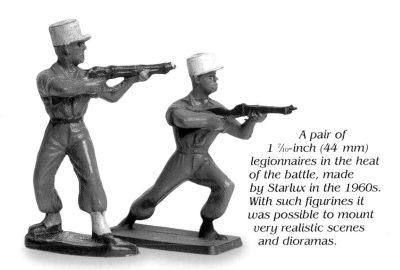

*A pair of
1 ⁷⁄₁₀-inch (44 mm)
legionnaires in the heat
of the battle, made
by Starlux in the 1960s.
With such figurines it
was possible to mount
very realistic scenes
and dioramas.*

Nº 3¹ Camp de Chalons. St. 60

Index, Acknowldgments and Addresses, and Bibliography

Index

The index features the main brands and artists that appear in the book.

Acknowledgements

*I would like to thank the following who made their collections
and memories available to me and generously shared their passions:*

Guy Devautour, for his knowledge of military uniforms, his precision, and availability.

Hervé Bernard, a fine historian and figurine enthusiast. He also creates figurines in the great Vertunni tradition. For more information, write to:
11, square Auguste Renoir
75014 Paris, France
Tel: +33 (0)6 63 96 51 42

François Binetruy, of the
Brocante de l'Orangerie
33, rue de l'Orangerie
78000 Versailles, France
Tel:+33 (0)1 39 50 28 74
Fax: +33 (0)1 39 02 15 02
François always has a large selection of toy soldiers in his Ali Baba–style boutique.

Jacques Roussel, who has one of the most extraordinary stores in Paris, displaying thousands of toy soldiers and figurines, new and old, each as impressive as the next.
34-37-38, galerie Montpensier
Jardins du Palais Royal
75001 Paris, France
Tel: +33 (0)1 40 20 00 11

Richard Souillé, a great collector of plastic toy soldiers—who does not, however, turn his nose up at plaster models. And his sons Oliver and Laurent, whose passion for figurines is absolute.

Doctor Simon, who had the great idea to retain his Quiralu and Vertunni toy soldiers from childhood and who allowed me to photograph them.

François Beaumont, of La Boîte à Soldats boutique, a trade center for antique toy soldiers.
28, rue Violet
75015 Paris, France
Tel and Fax: +33 (0)1 45 78 89 44

Jerry Meimoun, co-author, with Alain Thomas, of the beautiful Starlux book, which may be ordered by writing to:
18, rue de Rulles,
6720 Habay-la-Neuve (Belgium)

Raymond Oehl, a great enthusiast of antique toy soldiers, and a fount of knowledge.

Finally, and with great regret to not have met him, I would like to thank Christian Blondieau, who runs his store in the "Swiss Village" in Paris.
Le Képi Rouge
78, avenue de Suffren
75007 Paris, France
Tel: +33 (0)1 45 67 59 83
Both of his books, cited in the bibliography on page 379, were invaluable in their precision of detail, which demonstrates the depth and breadth of the author's passion for the subject.

Additional Addresses

Classic Toys
218 Sullivan Street
New York, NY 10012-1302
United States of America
Tel: +1 212-674-4434

See 12,000 toy soldiers on display at
The Forbes Magazine Galleries
62 Fifth Avenue
New York, NY 10011-8882

The Guards Toy Soldier Centre
The Guards Museum
Wellington Barracks
London SW1E 6HQ
United Kingdom
Tel (shop): +44 (0)20 7976 0805
Tel (office): +44 (0) 11897 33690
Fax: +44 (0)11897 33947
e-mail: shop@mklmodels.co.uk
www.mklmodels.co.uk

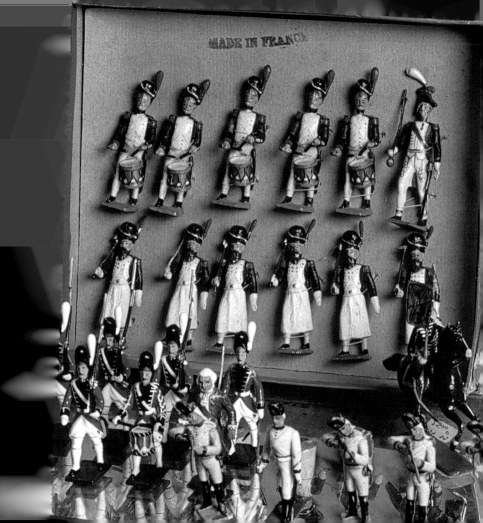

Bibliography

Alazet, R., J., Borsarello, H., and Giroud
Les Jouets Quiralu. Editions Jacques Grancher, 1995.

Berrafato, Laurent, ed. *Fantassin de la Grande Guerre*.
La Gazette des Uniformes, 1994.

Blondieau, Christian. *CBG, Soldats de Plomb & Figurines Civiles*.
Editions Le Képi Rouge, 1993.

Blondieau, Christian. *Petits Soldats, le Guide du Collectionneur*.
Editions Le Képi Rouge, 1996.

Hourtoulle, F.-G. *Borodino, the Moskova: the Battle for the Redoubts*.
Trans. Alan McKay. Paris: Histoire et Collections, 2000.

Kurtz, Henry I., and Burtt R. Ehrlich. *The art of the toy soldier*.
New York: Abbeville Press, 1987.

Meimoun, Thomas and Jerry. *Starlux*.
Published by the authors, 2000.

Opie, James. *Collecting Toy Soldiers*.
New Cavendish Books, 1987.

Ryan, Edward. *Paper Soldiers*. Golden Age Editions, 1995.

In the same collection

Collectible Pocket Knives
by Dominique Pascal
ISBN: 2-0801-0550-7

Collectible Wristwatches
by René Pannier
ISBN: 2-0801-0621-X

Collectible Fountain Pens
by Juan Manuel Clark
ISBN: 2-0801-0719-4

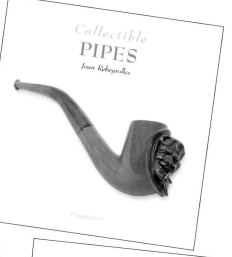

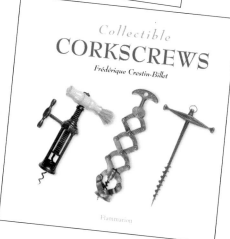

Collectible
MINIATURE
PERFUME BOTTLES

Anne Breton

Flammarion

Collectible
PLAYING CARDS

Frédérique Crestin-Billet

Flammarion

Collectible
SNOWDOMES

Lélie Carnot

Flammarion

Collectible Miniature Perfume Bottles
by Anne Breton
ISBN: 2-0801-0632-5

Collectible Playing Cards
by Frédérique Crestin-Billet
ISBN: 2-0801-1134-5

Collectible Snowdomes
by Lélie Carnot
ISBN: 2-0801-0889-1

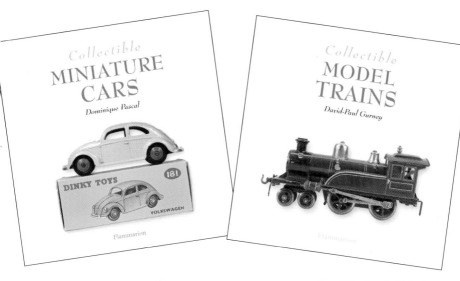

Collectible Miniature Cars
by Dominique Pascal
ISBN: 2-0801-0708-6

Collectible Model Trains
by David-Paul Gurney
ISBN: 2-081-1142-6

Photographic credits

DISCARD